The Havana Habit

Yale UNIVERSITY PRESS NEW HAVEN & LONDON

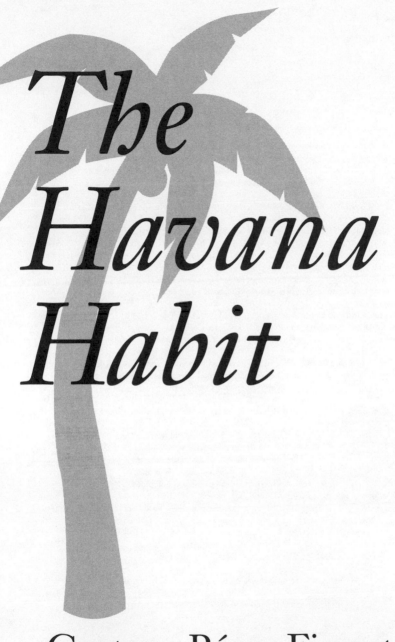

The Havana Habit

Gustavo Pérez Firmat

Yale University Press books may be purchased in quantity for educational, business, or promotional use. For information, please e-mail sales.press@yale.edu (U.S. office) or sales@yaleup.co.uk (U.K. office).

Set in Janson type by Integrated Publishing Solutions. Printed in the United States of America.

Library of Congress Cataloging-in-Publication Data
Pérez Firmat, Gustavo, 1949–
The Havana habit / Gustavo Pérez Firmat.
p. cm.
Includes bibliographical references and index.
ISBN 978-0-300-14132-0 (clothbound : alk. paper) 1. United States—Civilization—Cuban influences. 2. Cuba—In popular culture. 3. Popular culture—United States. 4. Popular culture—Cuba. 5. National characteristics, Cuban. 6. Cuba—Social life and customs. 7. Havana (Cuba)—Social life and customs. 8. Americans—Travel—Cuba—History. I. Title.
E169.12.P483 2010
306.0973—dc22 2010017498

A catalogue record for this book is available from the British Library.

This paper meets the requirements of ANSI/NISO Z39.48–1992 (Permanence of Paper).

10 9 8 7 6 5 4 3 2 1

For Mary Anne

Cuba—there's magic in the name alone.
—Lawrence Tibbett in *The Cuban Love Song* (1931)

Contents

Acknowledgments

This is a short book that was long in the making, and I owe a debt of gratitude to many people and institutions. The germ of the book was contained in a lecture I delivered at the Center for Free Inquiry of Hanover College in 2003. Since then, I've had the opportunity to develop my ideas before audiences at Dickinson College, Western Michigan University, the University of Delaware, Marist College, and the University of Louisville. The Cristóbal Díaz Ayala Collection at Florida International University provided not only access to its rich holdings on Cuban music but a travel fellowship that allowed me to use them. Mayra Nemeth and Verónica Rodríguez, the curators of the Díaz Ayala Collection, went out of their way to point me to the relevant materials. The Institute of Latin American Studies at Columbia University also provided travel and research funds. David Frasier and Zach Downey of the Lilly Library at Indiana University kindly furnished copies of hard-to-find sheet music. As in the past, Esperanza de Varona, María Estorino Dooling, and Lesbia Varona of the University of Miami's Cuban Heritage Collection answered my queries promptly and efficiently.

Jorge Olivares once again performed the fraternal though not thankless task of reading another of my manuscripts. For many years Isabel Alvarez Borland, Roberto González Echevarría, Ricardo Castells, and Rolando Pérez have been my friends and interlocutors. Roberto's support of the project from conception to completion was crucial. John Koegel generously shared with me his vast knowledge of Latin American music. Tony Hyman, curator of the National Cigar Museum, did the same for cigar advertising and memorabilia. A Southern dinner with Lori Carlson and Oscar Hijuelos provided timely encouragement. Jonathan Brent believed in the book when it was little more than wishful thinking. Sarah Miller, my editor at Yale, saw it through to its present form with enthusiasm and care. Laura Jones Dooley was a tactful and precise copyeditor.

I would also like to acknowledge the contribution of the two readers for Yale University Press, whose mostly sensible suggestions I have mostly followed. The students in my undergraduate class on Cuba and the United States at Columbia have been a joy to teach and learn from. Finally, Mary Anne Pérez Firmat, thanks to whom I haven't had to set foot in a library in years, collaborated in the writing of this story—our story—in ways mentionable and unmentionable.

Introduction

SO NEAR AND YET SO FOREIGN

In *You'll Never Get Rich* (1941), the first of two musicals in which Fred Astaire teamed up with Rita Hayworth, Fred plays a Broadway dance director who agrees to put on a show at the army base where he is stationed. During the rehearsal, he instructs the stagehands: "I want a tree right here"—and a fake palm tree appears; "Bring me a house"—and a Spanish-style facade slides onto the stage; "Boys, now I want an ocean"—and the boys bring in the backdrop: a large image of the entrance to Havana harbor as viewed from the seaside avenue called El Malecón. Once the scenery is in place, Rita Hayworth appears, looking *señorita*-lovely in a sheer black dress with a ruffled skirt. Leaning against the palm tree, Fred launches into Cole Porter's "So Near and Yet So Far," whose lyric seems to allude both to Rita and to Havana.

Fig. 1. Still from *You'll Never Get Rich.* "YOU'LL NEVER GET RICH" Copyright 1941, renewed 1969 Columbia Pictures Industries, Inc. All Rights Reserved. Courtesy of Columbia Pictures.

After Fred sings, he and Rita dance the most elegant rumba ever captured on film (fig. 1).

Fred's creation of a mock Havana in a movie that otherwise has nothing to do with Cuba—he is about to be shipped off to Panama—not only puts on display American perceptions about Latin America—rhythmic, romantic, fickle—but illustrates the centrality of Cuba to these perceptions. No other Latin American nation has left as pervasive an imprint on this country's cultural landscape as that long island in the Caribbean. Jon Lee

Anderson, the author of a book about Che Guevara, puts it this way: "I think Cuba is part of our psyche, our own historical landscape, and it inhabits part of our imagination as no other place does."[1] Anderson is right. Few nations anywhere have enjoyed—and endured—as close a relationship with the United States. For more than two centuries, the two countries have been linked by what William McKinley in 1899 termed "ties of singular intimacy," a close but contentious relationship that has produced rapprochements, disappointments, misunderstandings, embargos, *embarques*, and, every once in a while, a military occupation. If Cubans have always regarded *los americanos* with a mixture of fascination, fear, lust, disdain, and envy, Americans, for their part, have looked on Cubans with mixed feelings of their own. Ever since John Quincy Adams compared the island to an apple ready to drop into the lap of the United States, Cuba has been the object, and sometimes the target, of American desires. For Americans, Cuba has been both mirror and mirage: a magnified reflection of domestic anxieties as well as a beckoning oasis of otherness.

In *America in the Movies*, Michael Wood has argued that cultural myths inhabit the back of our communal mind, a site at the edge of consciousness that nevertheless insistently begs for attention.[2] That has been Cuba's location, in the back of America's mind, always present if not always front and center, somewhat like the backdrop in *You'll Never Get Rich*. Another example: in Dashiell Hammett's novel *The Maltese Falcon*, Sam Spade whistles a song called "En Cuba." Sam is in San Francisco and his mind is on the bird, but the back of his mind is elsewhere: "in Cuba." The same thing happens to Brigid O'Shaughnessy, the girl with the bird, who also likes to whistle "En Cuba" (even though she has just returned from the Far East). The song didn't make it into the movie (perhaps because there was no such tune, though there were many like it), but Cuba did, since Sam Spade's office looks out on a nightclub named "Cubana." There it is again, literally in the background, its presence taken for granted, that back-of-the-mind country that bears a complicated resemblance, though a resemblance nonetheless, to the real thing. Unlike the priceless statuette, Cuba is not *rara avis* but backyard bird. It will show up again in Sam's favorite drink (bootleg Bacardi), as well as in Sidney Greenstreet's favorite smoke (Cuban coronas).

The Cuba of these movies—cardboard, neon, music, smoke, rum—is almost, but not quite, a fantasy island. I will call it a locale rather than a location—that is, a setting not bound by geography, a "there" without a "where," the kind of place that can materialize anyplace: on an army base near New York or a PI's office in San Francisco.

To understand American transactions with this locale, I have found it useful to isolate two distinct modes of intimacy, characteristic ways in which the United States has grasped things Cuban. According to Victor Segalen's classic definition, exoticism is the feeling that diversity stirs in us.[3] As a species of exoticism, American impressions of Cuba denude diversity of one of its usual conditions—distance. Detaching the foreign from the faraway, diversity from distance, this mode of intimacy embodies a "soft" exoticism, a tamer, less hazardous experience of otherness. During the 1920s, when more than half a million Americans visited the island, the playwright Basil Woon published a tourist guide entitled *When It's Cocktail Time in Cuba* (1928). His title sent complementary messages: in Cuba you can do what you can't in the States—drink to your heart's content; and yet in Cuba intemperance comes under the aegis of an eminently American institution—cocktail time. Even as the book insists that the island's main appeal lies in its "utter foreignness," it defangs foreignness by making it follow familiar routines. Indeed, Cuba's very name seemed to contain an American greeting, as in one of Irving Berlin's songs, also written during the Prohibition era: "I'll See You in C-U-B-A." Once again, the title laces familiarity with foreignness, for otherwise it would not be necessary to spell out the country's name. Cuba remains close but alien, "so near and yet so far."

In the 1930s and 1940s, the Cuban Tourist Commission capitalized on the singularity of Cuban-American ties with the slogan "So near and yet so foreign," in which the pun makes clear that the distance between the countries is cultural rather than physical, a matter of mores rather than miles (fig. 2). This has always been the American perception. Cuba is close but different, like a relative who doesn't resemble anyone else in the family. In the middle of the nineteenth century, Boston journalist William Henry Hurlbert recorded his first impression of Havana: "So it seems to me, that to have reached this stately panorama of Havana, we must have traversed many miles of longitude instead of a few degrees of latitude." James Steele, an American consul in Cuba in the 1870s, shared Hurlbert's sentiment: "You are only ninety miles from the winking lighthouses and sandy shore of Florida, but you have entered dominions as foreign, as different, as full of strangeness, as though you had sailed around the world to find them."[4] For Hurlbert and Steele, as for other nineteenth-century American travelers, Cuba was the Orient of the Americas—its shape that of a scimitar, its capital's architecture reminiscent of Baghdad's (as it happens, Cuba's easternmost province used to be called Oriente).

The impression of strangeness persists undiminished into the twentieth century. After observing Cuban customs—from courtship rituals to cockfights—the authors of *Havana Mañana* (1941) conclude that Cuba inhabits a different world altogether: "It seems incredible that this alien way of life has continued placidly so near our bustling American shores and yet so unchanged by them. Havana is two hours by plane from the U.S.A.; but it is so remote from the American pattern of living, it could well be on another planet."[5] That was—and is—Cuba's allure: it allows Americans to drop in on another planet (Planet Cuba), thereby quenching their wanderlust without having to wander. Even after the travel ban imposed in the 1960s, which severely cur-

HAVANA WITH PRICE TOURS
SO NEAR AND YET SO FOREIGN
90 Miles from Key West
VISIT
CUBA

Fig. 2. "So Near and Yet So Foreign." Poster by Conrado Massaguer for the Cuban Tourist Commission.

tailed the flow of American visitors, Cuba has remained the picturesque if odd next-door neighbor, someone one could visit and marvel at, like Ricky Ricardo on the *I Love Lucy* show.

And not only marvel at, but emulate. In *Week-End in Havana* (1941), one of the many Latin-themed musicals of the 1930s and 1940s, the title song promises that after spending a weekend in Havana, "you won't be the same any more." In the movie the two protagonists, played by Alice Faye and John Payne, bear out the lyric's promise: Payne discovers a more passionate self, a non-Latin "Latin" persona, while Faye evolves from salesgirl at Macy's to fiancée of a rich, eligible bachelor. The viewers who saw this movie in October 1941, just as the United States was about to be drawn into World War II, did not undergo literal transformations; nonetheless, they too were changed, if only vicariously, by the island's "tropical magic" (the title of the movie's ballad). Cuba offered the possibility of becoming someone else elsewhere, at least for a little while.

Because in back-of-the-mind Cuba time proceeds at a different pace, the viewer hardly notices that the weekend in Havana actually spreads out over two weeks or that John Payne goes to Miami and back in less time than it takes to dance a rumba. The fateful rhyme "Havana-mañana," exploited in countless songs (along with, less frequently, that of "Bacardi" and "tardy"), may or may not reflect the habits of deferral of people of Hispanic or Latin American origin, but it certainly speaks to the mode of existence of Cuba as locale. If you go to Havana, where it's always mañana, you will be traveling to a world governed by a special temporality, a notion that has acquired an excruciating poignancy in today's Havana, with its 1950s vintage Chevys rolling down narrow streets lined with decayed colonial buildings.

As poets and others have not tired of reminding us, one of the most unsatisfactory things about the world we live in is that time passes, people leave. Imagine a place where this does not happen: not just a "there" without a "where," but a "when" without a "then." We need such a place, if only because it doesn't exist. For the most part, back-of-the-mind Cuba, with a calendar composed entirely of holidays and weekends, is such a place.

In *Week-End in Havana*, the covert plot of the movie, which runs parallel to the boy-gets-girl story, pits tight, uptight Jay Williams (Payne), who goes to Cuba to prevent his ship line from being sued, against free-spending Monte Blanca (Cesar Romero), who is not only a "Latin Lover" but a compulsive gambler (not coincidentally, *monte* is a Spanish game of cards). At the end of the film, Monte dashes into a nightclub running away from the hoodlums to whom he owes money. He goes over to Jay and asks for five hundred dollars to save his life. Jay replies that Monte's life is not worth five hundred. Monte then counters with the last line in the script, "Well, make me an offer." Before Jay can answer, Monte gets swallowed up by the spectacular musical finale and joins Carmen Miranda in performing the title tune. Mañana-land, not money, saves Monte's life. Time is money, but while the weekend lasts, neither one matters.

Because the Cuba of *Week-End in Havana* is a tissue of conventions, a commonplace, it is impervious to change. Once a commonplace has lodged itself in a culture's psyche—or at least in this culture's psyche—it seems to perpetuate itself with little regard for real events. Since the commonplace trumps the historical place, American images and beliefs about Cuba have remained essentially the same for two hundred years, in spite of the social and political tempests that have battered the island. Revolution or no revolution, embargo or no embargo, the Cuba at the back of the American mind continues to furnish compensatory pleasures. As we shall see, contemporary ideas about Cuba have not abandoned habits of perception established many years before anyone had ever heard of Fidel Castro.

Of course, movies from the 1940s generally show us what we can't have because it doesn't really exist. The question, however, is which of the myriad things that we can't have Cuba supplies. For a century and a half, until relations with the United States turned sour, Cuba provided an escape, but of a particular kind. Fantasy is the stock-in-trade of films about foreign places, from *An American in Paris* to *Around the World in Eighty Days*, but it makes a difference in what direction one is heading. Travel to the south, to the tropics, conjures up a distinctive set of expectations. In the nineteenth century, when a young man went west, as Horace Greeley enjoined, he forayed into a space of unlimited opportunity where he could, as the second half of the phrase stated, "grow up with the country." *Go South, Young Man*, the title of Tony Martin's 1958 recording of Latin songs, offers a different kind of promise: not to grow up but to get away, not with the country but outside of it, and not by yourself but in the company of like-minded individuals. The Latin South is, first and foremost, the realm of the senses, a bazaar of bodily gratification staffed by happy, sociable hedonists. It's the place where American young men and women discover rum, rumba, and romance, the last mostly with each other, though on occasion romantic relations turn international. A word that recurs in songs and movies with Latin content is "down": *Flying Down to Rio*, *Down Argentine Way*, *Down Mexico Way*. It's not irrelevant that to "go down" is sexual slang. Going down, Northerners shed inhibitions imposed by their climate and customs. Like other tropical locales, Cuba is a pleasure island, an Eden for the sensually deprived.

It is well to remember that exoticism says as much about the exoticizing subject as about the exoticized object. As Dorothy Figueira explains it, the exotic is a mode of self-definition that allows a culture to understand itself by differentiation. Sultry Carmen Miranda makes demure Alice Faye stand out in relief, as does Cesar Romero with John Payne. But exoticism does not arise only from a desire for differentiation. Equally important is the complementary mechanism, projection—predicating of others qualities or impulses one represses in oneself. The Cuba of *Week-End in Havana* showcases behavior that not only diverges from the "American pattern of living," as the authors of *Havana Mañana* phrase it, but that this pattern discourages or forbids; for instance, the desire to spend one's time playing like Monte rather than working like Jay. Chronicling his visit to Havana in 1919, Joseph Hergesheimer concludes: "It was impossible to determine what I had seen of Havana and what was merely my reflected self."[6] What is true of Hergesheimer is true more generally of perceptions of Cuba, America's reflected self, enticing but ultimately undesirable: a nice place to visit, but you wouldn't want to live there. To "go south" is also what happens when an enterprise fails.

This is not to say, however, that Cubans have not been complicit in their exoticization. Even if the slogan "So near and yet so foreign" was the brainchild of some clever Madison Avenue adman, the rumbera was drawn by the Cuban cartoonist Conrado Massaguer, and the poster was part of a campaign by the Cuban Tourist Commission, which for several decades brightened American newspapers with images and descriptions of the "Exquisite Isle of Delight." In Massaguer's drawing, the invitation to "Visit Cuba" is inserted between the rumbera's legs, and the contours of her crotch mime the "V" in "Visit." Without some degree of reciprocity, there is no intimacy. The American idea of Cuba—what scholars of tourism call the "destination image"—was produced by collaboration. American perceptions respond to Cuban impressions, to the imprint Cubans have made on the United States. It has been a two-way, back-and-forth negotiation that cannot be explained unidirectionally as the imposition of a foreign idea. From José Martí to Fidel Castro, from Cesar Romero to Gloria Estefan, from fine cigars to mojitos, Cubans and things Cuban have captured the American imagination, which means that they have seized it. In so doing, they have participated in the invention of the locale that Americans, not without reason, label "Cuba." It may be that, at least in this instance, exoticism begins at home, with indigenous appraisals.

If soft exoticism allows Cuba to be foreign yet familiar, the other mode of intimacy turns the island into a movable feast. Composed in the early days of Prohibition, Berlin's "I'll See You in C-U-B-A" begins:

> Not so far from here
> There's a very lively atmosphere;
> Everybody's going there this year.

In Berlin's lyric, Cuba is not a country but an "atmosphere." The word will recur. "Miami Beach Rhumba," recorded by Xavier Cugat in the 1940s, tells the story of a girl who, determined to learn how to rumba, sets off for Cuba. But after she meets a Cuban caballero and spends the night dancing under palm trees that whisper "te quiero," she decides that she no longer has to go to Cuba, for she has already experienced "all its atmosphere" in Miami Beach.

Because an atmosphere, unlike a country, is portable, one does not need to travel to Cuba to visit Cuba. An article about the Cuban Pavilion at the 1939 World's Fair puts it this way: "Latin atmosphere is apparently strong enough to survive the most alien surroundings. . . . A comfortable atmosphere of mañana, or, freely translated, 'tomorrow will do as well as today,' prevails in the Cuban restaurant."[7] In the 1990s, half a century after the World's Fair, Aramis launched "a hypnotic new fragrance for men" called "Havana." The slogan: "Atmosphere rather than place." Capitalizing on the abiding allure of Cuba, the slogan mooted its inaccessibility to most Americans. If Havana is atmosphere rather than place, if its essence is an essence, a scent, it's everywhere in general and nowhere in particular. Forget the embargo: to visit Havana, it is enough to envelop oneself in the strong, fruity aroma.

The notion of atmosphere is a powerful tool in the assimilation of foreignness. Atmospherics is another mode of intimacy, a means of cultural appropriation that has the further advantage of keeping the appropriated object at bay. If soft exoticism brings the exotic close to home, atmospherics guarantees that the closeness will not become uncomfortable. An atmosphere both connects and insulates: connects in its reproduction of tokens of the foreign culture, but insulates in that these tokens take the place of a full-bodied immersion. Fundamentally a sensory hallucination, atmosphere fosters the illusion of transport so that one feels oneself to be in a faraway place without ever leaving home. Because it relies on illusion—"feel" for "real"—it offers acquaintance without contact, pleasure without risk, yet another way of being "so near and yet so far."

An atmosphere has the further advantage of reducing foreign languages to sound effects. Although "Miami Beach Rhumba" does not say so explicitly, what Miami Beach has over Cuba is the English language, the principal feature that distinguishes the song from Cuban music. In an atmosphere, the native language—say, Spanish—loses its denotative function and becomes ambient, aromatic, like those breezes that whisper "te quiero." The Spanish words in Latin-tinged American songs have no more—

but also no less—significance than the bongo beats or the syncopated rhythms.

This notion of atmosphere applied not only to Cuba. The first Cuban song to become a hit in the United States, in 1930, was a tune by Moisés Simons called "El manisero," in English "The Peanut Vendor." An ad for a popular radio program, *The Lucky Strike Hour*, included the following: "Those who have visited Cuba, Mexico or other Latin American countries, will find this atmosphere faithfully portrayed in a novelty, 'The Peanut Vendor,' to be performed by Lew White, organist, tonight." Other than the odd choice of instrument, what is notable is that, according to the writer, Cuba, Mexico, and the rest of Latin America share a common atmosphere. A couple of years later an item in the *Washington Post* announced the opening of Club Habana, a nightspot whose "atmosphere is very Mexican." In the La Conga Room, the bandsmen are "genuine Argentines" and their "pulsant congas and the dynamic decorations make you think you're somewhere near the River Plate." Also in D.C., a debutante ball at the Mayflower Hotel featured young ladies wrapped in Spanish shawls doing the tango in a "tropical atmosphere" while their escorts, "Spanish cavaliers," staged a mock bullfight.[8]

Instead of a continent with two languages, two dozen countries, and divergent musical traditions, Latin America is an "atmosphere" into which national differences evaporate. It is enough to watch a few of the so-called maraca musicals of the 1940s to verify that it made little difference whether the señorita was Cuban or Brazilian or whether the caballero was Mexican or Argentinean. In *Too Many Girls* (1940), the movie where Desi Arnaz first met Lucille Ball, Arnaz played the part of Manuelito, a young man from Argentina who beats on the conga drum. In *Week-End in Havana*, no one finds it odd that Carmen Miranda sings in Portuguese. The original title of *Down Argentine Way* (1941), the first musical inspired by Franklin D. Roosevelt's Good Neighbor Policy, was "Down in Rio." When the country was changed, Carmen Miranda remained, still singing in Portuguese (as ambient sound, Portuguese is indistinguishable from Spanish).

In the late 1950s and early 1960s one of the staples of American popular music was the long-playing record of songs with a Latin beat and an English-language lyric. These albums featured singing stars as well as lesser lights: Nat King Cole's *Cole Español* (1958); Mel Tormé's *Olé Tormé* (1959); Irving Fields's *Bagels and Bongos* (1959; Fields, the Jewish King of Latin Music, who composed "Miami Beach Rhumba," also wrote "Havanna Guilah"); Peggy Lee's *Latin ala Lee* (1960); Dean Martin's *Cha Cha de Amor* (1962) and *Dino Latino* (1963); and Doris Day's *Latin for Lovers* (1964). *Dino Latino* contains an English version of the old Cuban song "La paloma": "When I left Havana nobody saw me go, / except my little gaucho maid who loved me so." A gaucho maid in Havana is incongruous enough, but not less than the album cover, a sketch of Dean Martin dressed like a matador (fig. 3). Put it all together and this is the picture: an Italian-American

Fig. 3. Dean Martin, album cover, *Dino Latino*. Courtesy of Universal Music Enterprises.

crooner dressed like a Spanish bullfighter singing a song about an Argentine girl who lives in Havana.

Since an atmosphere has no history, no borders, no flag, atmospheric Latin Americanism turns Latin America into a continent of interchangeable parts. Removing the indicia of nationality to replace them with a crude version of what today we might call ethnicity, atmospherics breeds denationalization, the most important feature in American perceptions of Latin America. The Hollywood "Latin" of the 1930s and 1940s is a forebear of today's "Latino," which is one reason why contemporary America has so easily assimilated the notion of the nationless "Latino," a politically correct version of the old stereotype. This erasure of nationality is neatly summarized in a line from *Damn Yankees* (1958) when Lola, the Latin bombshell who gets whatever she wants, reveals that she hails from "somewhere generally in South America" (South American Lola also happens to be Miss West Indies). Under the pressure of atmospherics, Cuba blends into the generalized geography of Lola's pan-Latin "somewhere," a locale without a location.

Denationalization produces incongruities that, depending on one's mood and mindset, are either comical or insulting. In October 1932, for a "Bolero Ball" held at the Waldorf Astoria in New York City, the hotel was decorated "in Argentine fashion" and the show featured "Argentine dancers" and "Gaucho guitarists." A couple of years later, when bandleader Luis del Campo was headlining at a midtown nightclub, the *New York Times* remarked: "He is, they say, Chilean, and thereby qualified to conduct a show which leans toward rhumba rhythms."[9] Campo, incidentally, was Cuban. Perhaps more than any other country in Latin America, Brazil was denatured by atmospherics. In *Flying Down to Rio* (1933), the big ballad is a tango and the dance extravaganza, "Carioca," is a rumba. Some years later, in "A Rainy

Night in Rio," written for *The Time, the Place, and the Girl* (1946), "señoritas" have nowhere to "say sí sí." And in the 1960s, Paul Anka warbled macaronic Spanish in "Eso Beso," another samba knockoff.

But if in the American mind the specifically Cuban fades into the generically Latin, the opposite also happens: what is specifically Cuban is often construed as generically Latin. Cuba then functions as a proxy for Latin America as a whole—as in the *Lucky Strike Hour* ad, where "The Peanut Vendor," a Cuban *son*, evokes a homogeneous Latin "atmosphere." The tendency to view the entire continent through the filter of the Caribbean is also evident in the ubiquitous Cuban music that American advertisers use to pitch the most disparate products, from "cha-cha-Charmin" toilet paper to "sheerly cha-cha" nail polish. With the ubiquitous Caribbean rhythms in the background, national differences dissolve into the Havana-scented "Latin" atmosphere. Even the dramatic changes in Cuba over the past fifty years have not altered the island's mediating role in American transactions with Latinness.

Why Cuba rather than some other Latin American country has occupied the "Latin" slot in the American mind is an interesting question. Part of the answer has to do not only with the island's proximity but with its strategic value. Though less relevant today, during the last century Cuba's location at the entrance to the Gulf of Mexico provided an outpost from which to dominate the Caribbean (witness the Guantanamo Naval Base), as well as a point of access to the continental mainland. Another part of the answer has to do with the traditional Northeastern-centrism of American culture. When distances are measured from New York City rather than from Los Angeles, Havana is a lot closer than Mexico City. And related to this may be the racial and class makeup of Cuba, similar to that of the United States in the lack of a significant indigenous population and in the prevalence of whites in the middle and upper classes. As the author of a 1946 guidebook put it, without a hint of irony, "Cuba is the only Latin American country in which the North American is not constantly reminded that we killed off all our Indians."[10] In addition, Cuba is an island, and islands not only are territorially singular, but they have a special hold on the imagination, as every reader of Daniel Defoe or Robert Louis Stevenson knows. Thomas More's Utopia was an island, as was Atlantis.

My preferred explanation, however, has little to do with American politics or the Western literary imagination. In 1951 a piece in the *Washington Post* asked what it was that made Americans prefer Cuba to other "lovely islands and picturesque cities." After reviewing the possible reasons, the author concluded that Cuba's appeal comes down to one thing: *bilongo*. "'Bilongo' is atmosphere—a special kind of atmosphere which makes a city or country a nice place to visit or in which to live. It's a combination of everything—climate, scenery, nice neighbors and pleasant customs. And in Havana's case it should also include good food."[11] The definition is revealing but wrong, for *bilongo* (pronounced "bee-lón-go"), a term that originated in *santería* rituals, is an Afro-Cuban word for a hex. When someone sends "bilongo" your way, he puts you under a spell. Nonetheless, the author is right to the extent that Cuba's appeal lies in the magic of its atmosphere (in Spanish, its *ambiente*)—a beneficent spell that has held Americans in its thrall for two hundred years.

Every several decades, the United States discovers Cuba again for the first time. The occasion for the discovery can be a dance craze, a TV series, a revolution, cigars and spirits, or even a novel, as happened some years ago with Oscar Hijuelos's *The Mambo Kings Play Songs of Love* (1989). These repeated acts of discovery are remarkable for their uniformity. Regardless of conditions on the island, what the United States discovers in Cuba is always a complicated variation on the cliché of the "island paradise," a place that, because it is an island, exists apart from history. This is as true of nineteenth-century travel diaries as it is of Prohibition Era accounts of Havana "alcoholidays" or contemporary descriptions of Cuba as "the hippest island in the world." The variations are complicated because, as we shall see in the chapters that follow, this paradise is sometimes pictured as serpent-stung, a corrupt Eden where fallen Adams and Eves pursue illicit pleasures.

As René Wellek remarked years ago, national images are mostly national illusions: one country's exercise in wishful thinking about another (understanding that wishful thinking also includes thinking about things that we would rather not think about).[12] Because they are illusions—as the stage set is an illusion—American ideas about Cuba illustrate how ties of singular intimacy are wrapped around a core of sober assessments as well as of hyperbole, distortions, and fantasy. But just as I do not believe that back-of-the-mind Cuba was made in the United States alone, I do not subscribe to the view, increasingly widespread it seems, that American popular culture is an arm of the State Department. The Cuba of these pages is a locale that Cubans and Americans have imagined together, at times in agreement with and at times in defiance of the two countries' changeable political relations. There is something—call it *bilongo*—that draws Cuba and the United States together, as if the two countries and cultures complemented, perhaps completed, each other. To *my* mind, Fred's best partner was not Ginger but Rita.

ONE

America's Smartest City

Sooner or later, almost no one can escape going to Havana.
—*The New Yorker*, 1940

Although it may not be so any longer, for most of the last two centuries the Morro Castle was the most recognizable item of Latinamericana in the United States. Never mind that it was sometimes mistakenly called the Morrow Castle, perhaps because of the island's reputation for *dolce far niente*, or the Moro Castle, probably because of the Moorish influence on Havana's architecture. Cuba was Havana and Havana was El Morro. Its visage on countless postcards, the castle's beacon, towering above the narrow entrance to the harbor, instantly identified the location as Havana, the gayest city in the world. That the symbol of gaiety should have been a fortress built at the end of the sixteenth century to defend the city from British buccaneers exemplifies the transformation of Havana from "Key to the New World and Bulwark of the West Indies," the inscription on the city's coat of arms, to Paris of the New World, Monte Carlo of the Caribbean, Las Vegas of Latin America, and Pleasure Capital of the Western Hemisphere—as well as "America's Favorite Foreign City" and "the Smartest City in America" (the last epithet another creation of the Cuban Tourist Commission, which evidently did not mind annexing Havana to the United States).[1]

The proliferation of nicknames highlights the city's appeal to Americans, for whom the Cuban capital was so familiar that at times it did seem like an American city, not "La Habana" but "Havana." In the course of a hundred years—roughly between the 1850s and 1950s—Americans developed what Frederic Remington, a correspondent in Cuba during the Spanish-American War, called the "Havana habit," a custom that drew increasingly large numbers of Americans of all stripes—adventurers, tourists, businesspeople, movie stars, mobsters—to Cuba's capital. Some of them wintered there, while others came for a weekend or for only the day. As the habit spread, La Habana became two cities: the real-world settlement founded by Diego Velázquez de Cuéllar at the beginning of the sixteenth century, and a fantasy city, a pleasure dome with a life of its own that shared its location with the city of brick and stone. This was the Havana of travel books and tourist guides, of Tin Pan Alley songs and Hollywood musicals. Because this Havana was timeless, it had only an intermittent connection to the often truculent events that took place in the Cuban city. In the 1920s, one visitor called it "the first station this side of Utopia."[2] Utopia, literally, is no place.

But let's begin with the city of brick and stone. Originally founded on the southern coast of the island, La Habana was moved to its present location in 1519. Its full name is San Cristóbal de La Habana: the first part an homage to Cuba's discoverer, Cristóbal Colón; the second inspired by the name of the daughter of an Indian chief. At first, and for several decades, La Habana was a modest village with only a few hundred inhabitants. Essentially defenseless, it was the target of frequent raids by pirates who, however, did not find much of anything to seize. As the sixteenth century wore on, Spain recognized Havana's strategic position as the "key" to its New World possessions. Its spacious, narrow-necked harbor on the edge of the Gulf Stream made it an ideal meeting point for the gold-laden galleons returning from Mexico and South America. Twice a year, the Spanish fleet would gather in Havana to pick up supplies and prepare for the risky transatlantic journey. To make the city safe from the likes of Francis Drake (whose ferocity was signified by his Spanish nickname, El Draque, The Dragon), large, sturdy fortresses were built, the Morro Castle most prominent among them.

Although the Spanish crown believed Havana to be impregnable, a century later the British demonstrated otherwise. At war with Spain and France, England dispatched a force of several thousand, which included hundreds of American colonists, led by the earl of Albemarle. After a three-month siege, Havana fell into British hands. (Bloody as the siege was, Albemarle recalled looking at Havana through his spyglass and seeing the natives dancing in the streets.) The British stayed for less than a year, until Spain agreed to cede Florida to England in exchange for Havana.

Though short-lived, the British occupation was instrumental in shaping the city's future. Before the British took over, Havana, like other Spanish ports in the New World, had been permitted to trade only with Spain, a restrictive policy that benefited Spain but did little for its colonies. With the redcoats came free trade (and also, unfortunately, unfree trade: a bump in the importation of slaves). As an English possession, Havana gained access to North American markets and North American imports. Once the genie was out of the bottle, it could not be put back in. After Spain regained possession of the island, it had no choice but to slacken the prohibitions on foreign trade. In 1776 Spain opened trade from Cuban ports with the new American republic; in 1818 restrictions on foreign trade were lifted altogether. Yearly port entries went from a handful to several hundred. The expansion of trade brought to Havana, for the first time, immigrants and merchants from the United States and Europe, an influx of people and goods that made Havana the cosmopolitan city it has remained to this day.

After trade restrictions were eased, the United States quickly became Cuba's principal trading partner. Cuba offered sugar, coffee, and tobacco (a sweetener, a tonic, and a narcotic), as well as less common imports such as lottery tickets and *cocuyos*, Cuban fireflies, renowned for the brightness and duration of their beam. The fledgling American republic offered manufactured goods, foodstuffs, and technology—from gas lights for the streets to machinery for the *ingenios* or sugar plantations. Traveling through the Cuban countryside in the 1840s, William Cullen Bryant rode in a rail car made in Newark drawn by an engine made in New York worked by an American engineer.[3] By the middle of the nineteenth century, fully two-thirds of the hundreds of ships anchored in the Havana harbor at any one time flew the Stars and Stripes. As visitors liked to mention, all those masts made the harbor look like an American forest.

With trade and accessibility came the first stirrings of the Havana habit. In the 1840s and 1850s, several thousand Americans visited Havana every year, including such notables as future presidents Grover Cleveland and Ulysses S. Grant. In 1853 William Rufus King, Franklin Pierce's running mate, became the first vice president of the United States sworn in on foreign soil (tubercular, he had gone to Cuba for his health). Two years later, a hospital for Americans opened in Havana. Dozens of these visitors to Cuba recorded their impressions of the island. In addition to countless magazine and newspaper articles, between 1850 and 1899 more than seventy travel books about Cuba were published in the United States. These accounts reflect the full spectrum of opinions. Many travelers, charmed by the quaint, colonial city and the easygoing ways of its inhabitants, resorted to the paradisal metaphor, as did William Henry Hurlbert in

Gan-Eden: Pictures of Cuba (1854), whose title is Hebrew for Garden of Delights. To a "New Yorker in Havana," the city seemed "some fairy land, most jealously guarded by the mighty genii of the place from invasion by mortals of the outer world." The mighty genii are the Morro Castle, La Cabaña fortress, and other embattlements. Strolling through the city, with the scent of oranges and limes wafting in the air, this New Yorker thought that he was strolling through the groves of paradise. Another traveler, a Philadelphian, approached the city in a small boat: "And now, beneath the awning, sheltered from the sun's scorching rays, we enjoy the luscious sun-ripened orange, while our eyes feast upon the strangely beautiful scene before us: a scene more lovely than ever our imagination had pictured; a reality exceeding our brightest dream."[4]

Of course, ever since Columbus remarked that Cuba was the most beautiful land that human eyes had ever seen, the paradisal trope has shaped external (and to a large extent, internal) perceptions of the island. Furthermore, this comparison has been used apropos of all of the Americas, North as well as South. Columbus himself famously claimed, during his third voyage, to have reached the biblical Garden of Eden, which he placed near the mouth of the Orinoco River and described as having the shape of a woman's breast. In Cuba's case, however, the paradisal trope survived as metaphor long past the time when anyone took it literally, and throughout the nineteenth and twentieth centuries,

Cuba was insistently likened to the biblical Eden, sometimes seriously and sometimes in jest.

But not everyone who sailed or steamed past El Morro was impressed by Cuba's beauty. Because all of the city's refuse drained into the bay, its waters were usually filthy. As one traveler put it, Havana harbor was "a foul and seething cauldron" that was "smelt before it was seen." The city itself did not fare much better: "Havana is a great sewer, from which pestilential exhalations constantly arise. As soon as you enter this city, an insufferable smell assails you, and never quits as long as you remain in it" (what happened to the aroma of orange and lime?). The belief among Americans was that the stench emanated from the mixture of cigar smoke, garlic, and offal—a deadly combination. After some of the streets were paved in the 1830s, sanitary conditions improved somewhat, but the increasing population and poor drainage continued to make it an unsalutary place, the breeding ground of yellow fever, dengue, and other tropical diseases. In addition, insects were everywhere, especially the fearsome Cuban ants, "so large that they kill chickens by biting them in the throat." This plague produced one more nickname for Havana: "Queen of the Ant-hilles."[5]

For the Havana naysayers, the city's inhabitants were "deteriorated Spaniards," "strange-looking people" with an inflated sense of their own importance. As a rule, the men were noisy, insolent, and, most of all, lazy: "The Habaneros do nothing that they can do without doing." Their love for gambling, as well as the scarcity of good beef and the custom of having white rice (most of it imported from the United States) with every meal, also came in for frequent criticism. Even Cuban women, who had a reputation for beauty, did not escape unscathed. The same New Yorker who was enchanted by Havana observed that Cuban women not only dressed badly but were dull-witted, with "not one half that vivacity and esprit so characteristic of the French grisette." A fellow traveler was no more impressed by their appearance than by their wit: "The ugliness of the women amounts to a vice, and is unredeemed by any quality as sometimes palliates plainness of features. I have cried aloud for the beautiful Cuba, but in vain." A row of Cuban women sitting together, he added, is "an awful array of hideousness." Richard Henry Dana, the author of *To Cuba and Back* (1859), the most popular nineteenth-century book about Cuba, explained that mature Cuban women fell into "two classes, distinctly marked and with few intermediates: the obese and the shrivelled."[6]

For American travelers, the island was a contradiction, at once alluring and repulsive, pestilential as well as paradisal. In this respect, they reproduced the general conviction held by Europeans and Americans alike about the tropics: a place of bounteous beauty yet unfit for human habitation—or at least, for habitation by those hailing from northern climes. (According to James Steele, who wrote what may be the most vitriolic book ever published about Cuba, "Where the banana grows, men do not grow, unless they are black.")[7] Americans admired the island's scenery—its shimmering seas, its majestic palms, its luxuriant vegetation—yet cringed at the islanders and their customs (bullfights! serenades!). They were drawn to the capital, yet complained about the deplorable conditions they found there. Especially after slavery was abolished in the United States, its perpetuation in Cuba stained the island. Cuba was paradise, and Cuba was hell.

We should not forget that these appraisals of Cuba, whether glowing or damning, were refracted through the lens of prospective possession. Like John Quincy Adams and Thomas Jefferson before him, throughout the nineteenth century many Americans believed that the acquisition of Cuba was the natural consequence of the manifest destiny of the United States. As the *New York Sun* put it, "Give us Cuba and our possessions are complete." During the heyday of expansionist fever in the 1840s, even freedom-loving Walt Whitman endorsed Cuba's "speedy annexation," stressing the economic benefits it would bring to the Union.[8] These sentiments eventuated in several offers of purchase. In 1848, the year that Mexico lost a large chunk of its territory to the United States, James Polk offered Spain a hundred million dollars for Cuba. He was turned down. In 1854, Franklin Pierce upped the offer to one hundred and thirty million, an initiative endorsed by his successor, James Buchanan, but they too were turned down. Although the Civil War ended the talk of annexation for a while, Ulysses Grant renewed efforts to buy the island, and once again Spain wasn't interested, partly out of national pride and partly because the price wasn't high enough. Finally, in the months leading up to the Spanish-American War, William McKinley tried to stave off the conflict by offering three hundred million dollars for Cuba. Not long after he was turned down, Teddy Roosevelt and his Rough Riders were charging up San Juan Hill.

In addition to American efforts to acquire the island, Cuban annexationists, among them slave-owning planters who envisioned Cuba as part of the Confederacy, attempted to topple the colonial regime. The most serious plots were hatched by Narciso López (1797–1851), a Venezuelan-born general who had fought for the Spanish crown against the forces of Simón Bolívar. When he arrived in Cuba, López quickly fell out with Spanish authorities and began conspiring against them. After a botched attempt at internal revolt, López went into exile in the United States, where he joined ranks with the *filibusteros*, the name given by Spaniards to those who sought to overthrow the colonial regime by mounting raids on the island. In 1859, with soldiers recruited from Louisiana and other southern states, López organized a filibustering expedition, which was soon defeated. Again he escaped to the United States and assembled another expedition of five hundred men, a majority of them Americans (including the son of the U.S. attorney general), which landed a few miles west of Havana, but once again the filibusters were routed by the Spanish. This time López was captured and executed in Havana before a large crowd. One of the ironies of Cuban history is that the man who died fighting for the annexation of the island helped to design the Cuban flag. Known as *la bandera de la estrella solitaria*, the lone star flag, it bears a not accidental resemblance to the flag of Texas, the lone star state.

Because of the debate about annexation, the American travelers went to the island not just to enjoy themselves or convalesce in the warm climate but to inspect a potential addition to the Union. For this reason, praise of the majestic beauty of El Morro is often accompanied by an assessment of the fortress's defenses (the consensus: they would crumble before a cannonade from American battleships); and descriptions of Cuba's rich soil mention how much more these lands would yield if tended by American hands. So it is, for example, that the novelist Maturin Ballou, the author of another widely read travel book, *Due South* (1885), after extolling the "Eden of the Gulf," concludes: "Cuba is indeed a land of enchantment, where nature is beautiful and bountiful, and where mere existence is a luxury, but it requires the infusion of a sterner, a more self-reliant, self-denying and enterprising race to test its capabilities and to astonish the world with its productiveness." In contrast, William Henry Hurlbert, who shared Ballou's view of Cuba as an Eden, nevertheless worried that a barefooted, barefaced Cuban peasant "might perhaps, at no distant day, be inflicted upon our own unfortunate Congress, as a representative from the sovereign State of Cuba!"[9]

Whatever their outlook, the travelers who recorded their impressions made Havana familiar, a back-of-the-mind presence that no longer needed to be described in detail. As someone pointed out, "The city of Havana has been so often described that its streets, its shops, its customs, its houses, its family and social life, are as familiar to most American readers as those of one of our own cities." Or consider this conversation between two friends:

"Let us get away from this inhospitable climate, and take refuge in some suburb."

"In what suburb can we find a more decent temperature?"

"In Havana."

"What Havana?"

"Havana in Cuba."

"Do you call that a suburb of New York?"

"Well, it's nothing else. It is right at our doors—only four days distant, and that's nearer than Albany was to New York a hundred years ago."[10]

This was in 1883. In fifteen years, Americans would not only be visiting this suburb of New York, they would be living there.

■

Although Havana was blockaded by the American navy during the Spanish-American War (in truth the Spanish-Cuban-American War), no battles were fought in it or for it. Still, the war and its aftermath diminished the number of visitors to the city, which was still beset by poor drainage, inadequate communications and transportation, and an insufficient supply of fresh water. During the American occupation between 1898 and 1902, these problems began to be remedied, and one of the city's landmarks, the seaside avenue called El Malecón, was constructed. Nonetheless, for years after the war, when Americans thought of Cuba, they did not visualize "gay and splendid" Havana but scenes from the conflict: the sinking of the *Maine* (remember?); the daring rescue of Evangelina Cisneros, the most beautiful girl in Cuba; the annihilation of the Spanish fleet in Santiago de Cuba; the charge up San Juan Hill; the famous "message to García" delivered by an intrepid American soldier. After the war, Parker Brothers released several board games commemorating the victory over Spain, among them "War in Cuba" and "The Siege of Havana," while John Philip Sousa toured the country with a musical extravaganza, "The Trooping of the Colors," that exalted American patriotism.

Two decades had to pass before Havana once again became something like a suburb of New York. To this day, when Americans think of Havana, they visualize a place that was half-discovered, half-invented, in the 1920s. That this happened when it did was crucial, for during this decade the United States underwent what Edmund Wilson characterized as "the shock of recognition," a moment of national assertion when—as Wilson phrased it—"minds and imaginations were exploring in all directions." Cuba, and particularly Havana, was one of those directions: the last great American frontier, in the words of the novelist James Gould Cozzens.[11] As America discovered itself it discovered Havana, which may be another way of saying that it discovered what it was missing. Havana endorsed American ways, but it also defied them. Although the Platt Amendment had made Cuba a protectorate of the United States in 1903, cultural ties and tensions superseded politics. Here was an Americanized city that offered a reprieve from America. If not quite a suburb of New York, the Cuban capital was a commonplace, an instantly recognizable locale that existed within the United States as well as outside it. Although it may be an exaggeration to say that in the 1920s Havana became America's id, the city represented an uninhibited alternative to the legacy of Puritanism.

A convergence of events—happy or unhappy, depending on one's viewpoint—conspired in the timing of this discovery. The prosperity of the 1920s gave Americans the means and time to travel. Upward mobility enabled horizontal mobility, as more and more Americans began to take vacations. In addition, the development of efficient means of transportation, particularly air travel, made it easier to get on the move. It was in 1920 that a "flying boat" first took passengers to Cuba; in 1927 Pan American Airways established regular service between Key West and Havana. Instead of making the trip by hopping on a ship, as Irving Berlin had recommended in "I'll See You in C-U-B-A," now it was possible to hop on a Pan Am Clipper and make the same trip not in four days but two hours. The "Havana Special" took winter-weary Northerners by train from New York to Miami, where they boarded the seaplane to Havana.

But clearly the most important factor in Havana's prominence was the ratification of the Eighteenth Amendment. With Prohibition in place, the city became an oasis for the thirsty. The jokes about Cuba as the "Rumhound's Paradise" or "El Dorado of Personal Liberty" were endless. A Havana vacation was not a holiday but an "alcoholiday." In Cuba, it was said, all roads led to Rum. If the Platt Amendment made Cuba free, it was also said, the Eighteenth Amendment made the island indispensable. And this is the *New Republic's* portrait of the typical American tourist: "As he staggers on board ship, his pockets filled with those little bottles of rum which he fondly, and vainly, imagines will escape the custom's inspector's eye, he looks backward as Adam toward Eden."[12] Revisiting the paradisal metaphor, this essay gives us a hungover Adam and a Garden of Eden transformed into a cocktail bar.

Recognition, literally, is a knowing again, re-cognition. But the Havana that hundreds of thousands of tourists—eager conventioneers, bored businessmen, casino-starved gamblers, middle-class couples with a taste for adventure—got to know again during the Jazz Age was not the same city that Americans had visited throughout the nineteenth century. In the years during and after World War I, Havana underwent a makeover. The sharp rise in the price of sugar created an unprecedented economic boom in Cuba, a five-year period (1915–1920) known as La Danza de los Millones, "The Dance of the Millions" (in Cuba, even pesos dance), during which the per capita wealth of the island was the highest in the world. With money readily available, developers in and around Havana dug sewers and put up hotels, built racetracks and golf courses, carved out lakes and sculpted fountains, and then invited bankers and movie stars to enjoy them and spread the word about the glistening Queen of the Caribbean. Havana became a city of contrasts, a blend of old and new. The quaint colonial city with its fortresses, cathedrals, and narrow streets was still there, the Old World atmosphere ("Europe overnight") enhanced by the large immigration of Spaniards, especially from Galicia, during the first two decades of the century.[13] But inside and outside Old Havana a new city was emerging, a modern metropolis that reflected the tastes and aspirations of Cuba's middle and upper classes.

For the rest of the 1920s, as tourism flourished, so did the city. By the end of the decade, the city's population surpassed half a million (in 1900 it had been a little over two hundred thousand). Motor cars, including thousands of *fotingos* or taxis, rumbled down El Malecón. American visitors no longer had reason to complain about the lack of adequate accommodations. Near venerable fixtures like the Hotel Inglaterra—the favorite hangout of American correspondents during the Spanish-American War—now stood several modern hotels: the Sevilla Biltmore (where jazz was first played in Cuba), the Royal Palm, the Lincoln, the Ritz, the Almendares (with a ticker relaying quotes from the New York Stock Exchange), and the "smartest" of all, the Hotel Nacional, whose twin Mediterranean towers fronted the ocean. It was also during these years that an old café was reborn as Sloppy Joe's, the watering hole for several generations of American tourists.

The Presidential Palace, with interior decoration by Louis Comfort Tiffany, was completed in 1920. The capitol building, modeled on the one in Washington but rising a foot taller, was finished ten years later. El Malecón was extended westward to the elegant suburbs of Vedado and Miramar, with their Art Deco mansions and lush tropical greenery. The *Maine* monument, whose bronze figures were sculpted by the same artist who carved the heads on Mount Rushmore, was completed during these years. The Cuban passion for gambling still found an outlet in games of all kinds, from jai alai to cockfighting. For those who preferred table games, the Gran Casino Nacional, which had its gala opening on New Year's Eve, 1926, offered the usual complement: roulette, lucky seven, big six, baccarat. At the entrance, the visitor was greeted by a fountain where eight nude nymphs writhed in ecstasy (years later, after the casino was demolished, the fountain was moved to the Tropicana nightclub, where it now resides). And, of course, there was the Havana lottery, famous already in the nineteenth century, which (like cockfighting) had been banned during the American occupation but (again like cockfighting) had been revived not long after the Americans left.

In January 1928, at the height of the tourist boom, *Life* published a "Havana Number" to coincide with Calvin Coolidge's visit to Cuba. Although Silent Cal traveled to the island on official business (to address the Pan American Conference), he brought with him a large retinue of politicians, businessmen, and celebrities. Included in his party—and it was a party—was Will Rogers, who on disembarking in Havana promptly appointed himself "unofficial ambassador of ill will." *Life* capitalized on President Coolidge's visit by dedicating its Havana number "to the Cuban Spirit of Liberty, and may it remain forever at our disposal." For the editors of *Life*, the Cuban Spirit of Liberty inhered in the liberty of Americans to consume spirits, a belief pictured in a cartoon of two Americans in a bar agreeing that it was a good idea "to give Cubans their freedom" (it didn't matter that Cuba was still subject to the Platt Amendment, which empowered the United States to intervene at will in Cuban affairs). And this is their toast:

So here's to Havana,
And here's to Bacardi—
It falleth like manna
On weakling and hardy.[14]

Designed by the prominent cartoonist Conrado Massaguer, the cover of *Life* featured a winsome señorita in front of a large Cuban flag (fig. 4). Her hands hold open a Spanish fan that, instead of the usual floral motifs, displays images associated with tourism: an airplane, a car, a sailboat, a racehorse, golfers, swimmers, jai alai players, and several cocktail glasses tilting this way and that, as if serving invisible tipplers. But the ample fan hides

Fig. 4. Cover of *Life*, Havana Number, January 19, 1928.

no less than it reveals, since it covers up the chest of the bare-shouldered girl, leading the viewer to surmise that the sights on the fan conceal equally enticing attractions behind it. There is something of the tease in the way the señorita tilts her head, smiles, and covers herself, as if performing a Spanish fan dance intended to titillate as well as inform.

Massaguer's drawing cleverly denotes Havana's twin appeal as playland and museum. The señorita and her fan bespeak the colonial past, while the sights on the folds of the fan evoke the modern city: "For if the town was old, it was young too. Its perennial freshness, and the ease with which it wore its black mantilla and its roguish rumba ruffles made it distinctive."[15] Replace the mantilla with the fan, and this description, culled from a crime novel published in 1944 (*Mr. Angel Comes Aboard*), captures Havana's time-warping allure. Then as now, part of the charm, the bewitching foreignness of Havana resides in its preservation of relics from another time and place. The señorita herself is a retrofitted "Massa-Girl," the chic flapper that Massaguer drew throughout the 1920s for the magazine *Social*, which chronicled Cuban high-life. (The term "Massa-Girl" not only punned on the author's last name, but on the Cuban slang for flesh, "masa").

In another of Massaguer's illustrations for the Havana number, the Massa-Girl reappears, now holding a cocktail shaker rather than a fan. With a flirtatious wink, she says: "Shake hands with Havana" (fig. 5). On the cover, dressed in Spanish style with

Fig. 5. "Shake Hands with Havana." *Life*, Havana Number, January 19, 1928.

a flouncy skirt and a flower in her hair, the Massa-Girl is in costume, perhaps as she would be during carnival. In real life, behind or between the covers, she is a thoroughly modern Millie, or maybe a Cuban Sally Rand. The question remains: Is Havana the cocktail or is Havana the girl? It seems to be both. To shake hands with Havana one shakes a cocktail, or perhaps one shakes the sexy señorita, herself a Havana number.

A few months after the *Life* issue, the playwright Basil Woon published *When It's Cocktail Time in Cuba* (1928), whose first chapter bears the title "Have One in Havana." At the end of the book, the author appends "A Lover's Lexicon: First Aid to Romance in Havana." One of the phrases in the lexicon: "¿Cuánto es?" (How much?). It's clear that it wasn't only cocktails that could be had in Havana. In his autobiography, Hoagy Carmichael relates that his rumba "One Night in Havana" was inspired by a "Havana B-girl" whom he met during a night of tropical revelry. (The Havana B-girl, however, turned out to be from South Dakota.)[16]

Life's Havana number also included a "Dream's Eye View of Havana," a two-page map of the city seen through American eyes (fig. 6). Superimposing American perceptions and fantasies on the city's landmarks, the map furnishes a striking illustration of the distinction between location and locale, physical fact and tourist fiction. To be sure, there is overlap between the two, but it is the tourist's perspective that dominates, overlaying Cuban reality like a distorting lens. In the belief that Havana is all of Cuba (an impression shared by many Cubans, which is why Miami has a Little Havana instead of a Little Cuba), the map relocates San Juan Hill to the outskirts of the capital and the bay of Santiago de Cuba, where the Spanish fleet was destroyed, to Havana harbor. Cubans known to Americans, like the baseball star Adolfo Luque and the chess champion José Raúl Capablanca, find a place on the map, as do tourist attractions alternating old and new. Alongside the cathedral and the National Theatre, one finds the racetrack, the jai alai *frontón,* and the baseball stadium (where you can't tell the players without a guitar).

Exemplifying American attitudes toward Cuban sexual mores, the map also shows an iron-grilled colonial mansion that looks every bit like a cage, with a sign on the roof that cautions, "Don't feed the señoritas." Down the street another sign warns slow-moving Spaniards to keep right. In the bay, near a wind-up battleship (the Cuban navy), a couple of inebriated Americans swim past the Morro Castle's lighthouse, magically transformed into a traffic signal, and scream out, "I'll see ya ta morro!"

The map illustrates how the replacement of the nineteenth-century traveler with the twentieth-century tourist, and of La Habana with Havana, further complicated Cuba's image as a tropical paradise. For the tourist who traveled to Havana in the 1920s, Cuba remained a Garden of Delights, but with one qualification: it had become a post-lapsarian Eden, a garden of sensual delights, an earthy as well as earthly paradise. If in the nineteenth century paradisal imagery coexisted uneasily with the horrors of slavery, in the twentieth the taint of slavery gave way to the temptation of the forbidden, be it in the shape of cocktail shakers or Massa-Girls. As one tourist guide phrased it, Cuba is the place where "conscience takes a holiday." Even before the flood of tourists, warning bells had begun to sound among teetotaling Americans. In December 1919, a few weeks before Prohibition was to take effect, the Reverend Samuel Guy Inman, an

Fig. 6. "Dream's Eye View of Havana." *Life*, Havana Number, January 19, 1928.

iew of Havana

influential religious leader who later helped craft Roosevelt's Good Neighbor Policy, cautioned that Cuba was about to become "a sort of national cocktail route" for alcohol-deprived Americans. Alarmed that thousands of his compatriots had already requested passports to go to Cuba, Inman called for a fund-raising effort to establish evangelical centers in Havana that would "combat the evil." To which the Cuban consul general in the United States responded archly that, if Americans were to raise such a fund, they would probably spend it on daiquiris and lottery tickets.[17]

No one sounded the alarm louder than G. L. Morrill (1857–1928), a Minneapolis minister who under the pen name of the Reverend Golightly published a series of anti-Cuban and anti-Latin screeds with such titles as *Rotten Republics* (1916), *The Devil in Mexico* (1917), *The Curse of the Caribbean* (1920), and *Sea Sodoms* (1921) (a phrase Lord Byron had used apropos of Venice, another decadent paradise). According to Golightly, if God made Cuba, the Devil contributed Havana. The city where "bad people go to have a good time," Havana is "a Fool's Paradise—a lunatic limbo for people with loud clothes, lots of money, loose morals, and light hearts." Reprising the views of some nineteenth-century travelers, the reverend thought no more highly of Cubans than he did of tourists: "Too often the C in Cuban character stands for cupidity, carnality, crookedness, cabals, charlatanism, cursing, and contempt for Americans."[18] But Golightly was not above illustrating the carnality of Cubans with carnality of his own: snapshots of bare-breasted Cuban women, mostly black.

The dream's-eye view of Havana as licentious paradise, a combination greenhouse, clubhouse, and whorehouse, produced many representations of Havana as a seductive woman, like the one on Massaguer's cover. Paradisal imagery, like nature imagery more generally, has been conventionally construed as female, as Columbus made clear when he compared the Garden of Eden to a woman's breast. In Cuba's case, the feminization underscored the island's reputation for sensuality. In *Gan-Eden*, Hurlbert had called Cuba a "fair Odalisque" and the "luxurious daughter of the South," where the adjective "luxurious" evokes the Spanish word for lust, *lujuria*. Moreover, from the time of the city's founding, the legend about the beautiful Taíno princess had given Havana a female identity (*La* Habana), a connection exploited endlessly in tourist guides and travelogues. Describing Havana in 1920, Joseph Hergesheimer called it "a vision in blanched satin with fireflies in her hair." A year later, Basil Thompson compared the lights on El Malecón to "a diamond necklace about the throat of a dusky Aphrodite" (the adjective a not-so-subtle allusion to Cuba's racial mix). Another writer likened the city to a "confident siren" whose name rhymed with that of Émile Zola's Nana (who was a prostitute). The female authors of *Havana Mañana* echoed these male writers: "Havana is like a woman in love. Eager to give pleasure, she will be anything you want her to be—

exciting or peaceful, gay or quiet, brilliant or tranquil. What is your fancy? She is only anxious to anticipate your desires, to charm you with her beauty." Reading this passage one wonders whether Havana is a woman in love or rather a woman for sale, for the sentences waver uncomfortably between suggestions of courtship and prostitution, suggestions no less explicit in the chapter about Cuban night life in another guidebook: "Havana Sells Her Night." Even the mayor of Havana assured the presumptively male tourist that "nothing will be done to interfere with his pleasure."[19]

The stress on the seamy side of Havana nightlife—the peep shows, bordellos, and cellar dives—eventually congealed into the notion that the city was the "whorehouse of the Caribbean," a cliché that, like others, loses its grain of truth in an ocean of exaggeration. At any given time during the first half of the last century, there were several thousand prostitutes in Havana, but in this respect it was no different than other port cities or tourist resorts, in the United States and elsewhere (the difference, perhaps, was that Cubans have never made a virtue of discretion). According to an essay in the *Saturday Evening Post*, Havana was "cynical and sinful . . . a tropical version of the old Pompeii." (Another cliché: a century earlier James Steele had complained that Havana was "as rich, as wicked, as frivolous, as was Pompeii.") Magazines catering to a male audience, like *Stag* and *Eye*, were more explicit, describing the city as a man's town "where anything goes in plain and fancy sinning."[20] They accompanied these stories with cheesecake photographs of which the Reverend Golightly would have been proud.

Most Americans, however, did not read *Stag* or visit Havana. For them, the Havana habit was a mental habit. By the 1930s, the images of Havana in the back of the American mind arose not from firsthand acquaintance but from movies, songs, radio programs, and the ubiquitous ads of the Cuban Tourist Commission, which extolled the Exquisite Isle of Delight in language even more florid than the Massa-Girl's skirt. The Havana of music and film and tourist brochures became the truly inescapable city, the one Americans could visit without ever setting foot on El Malecón. Havana, rather than La Habana, was an imagined habitat, a locale created and re-created in such films as *Rumba*, *Week-End in Havana*, and *Holiday in Havana*, and in songs with titles like "Havana Heaven" and "Havana for a Night." Whatever La Habana was like in reality, Havana was a city that had not yet lost its innocence, a Massa-Girl with nothing to hide, whose name attached itself not only to fine cigars, as had been the case for two centuries, but to colors (Havana brown, the shade of the wrappers of Cuban cigars; Havana gray, the color of their ash) and fashion (Havana heels)—not to mention countless bars, restaurants, and nightclubs in every corner of this country.

Recorded by Desi Arnaz in 1949, "Ah-bah-nah, Coo-bah," provides a list of improbable events that occur only in Havana: the mystery lady at the masquerade turns out to be your wife; the rumba dancers learned their moves from Arthur Murray; the star baseball player Miguelito Ronaldo is actually "O'Bryan of the Brooklyn bums." In this magic city, where illusion reigns, all things Cuban are fake, even the Cubans. One can construe the lyric as a commentary about the ongoing Americanization of Havana, which has all but replaced indigenous culture (even the cigar-rollers smoke Chesterfields). But "Ah-bah-nah, Coo-bah," as the phonetic spelling suggests, is a locale designed for Americans, a cultural site rather than a historical city, dreamscape rather than landscape. This is why, as Desi brags in the refrain, "anything at all can happen in Habana, Cuba." Anything can happen, because nothing ever has.

TWO

A Little Rumba Numba

It seems as though there is always bad news coming from Cuba.
This year it was the revolution, and last year it was Cuban music.
—*Life* (1933)

In the 1940s, a song like Arnaz's "Ah-bah-nah, Coo-bah" was sometimes called a "latune," that is, a tune with a Latin beat but an English-language lyric. Although latunes drew on a variety of Latin American genres, Cuban rhythms prevailed, particularly the rumba (or rhumba), an elastic term that included up-tempo *sones* as well as languid boleros, and bore only a distant relation to the Afro-Cuban *rumba.* Cole Porter, who regarded himself as a "self-adopted Latin," wrote many rumbas, among them some of his classics: "In the Still of the Night," "Night and Day," "I've Got You under My Skin," and "Begin the Beguine" (which, as John Storm Roberts once remarked, should have been called "Begin the Bolero").[1] Porter was not alone. At one time or another, most of Porter's contemporaries—Irving Berlin, George Gershwin, Hoagy Carmichael, Harold Arlen, Johnny Mercer—

contributed to the latune songbook. Porter's 1941 stage musical, *Let's Face It*, contained a song whose title applied to many of his and his contemporaries' compositions: "A Little Rumba Numba."

In addition to original songs, the latune repertoire included Anglophone renditions of Cuban standards like "Canto Siboney" and "Mamá Inés," both of which became popular in the early 1930s. At the end of the decade, Ernesto Lecuona's "Say Sí Sí" ("Para Vigo me voy") sold over a million copies. In 1940, his "The Breeze and I" ("Andalucía") reached the top spot on *Your Hit Parade*, as did Artie Shaw's interpretation of "Frenesí." The following year, five different versions of "Perfidia" were top-fifteen hits, and during the 1940s, a war-weary nation found solace in sentimental songs like "Amapola," "Bésame mucho," "María Elena," "You Belong to My Heart" ("Solamente una vez"), and "Always in My Heart" ("Estás en mi corazón"), which not only earned a nomination for an Academy Award, but—more significantly—was featured in a Porky Pig cartoon, "Swooner Crooner" (1944).

Latunes are often silly, but they can also be ingenious and, on occasion, surprisingly artful. At its best, the fusion of Latin beats and English syllables engenders songs gracefully poised on the cultural border of Anglo- and Latin America, somewhere between Tin Pan Alley and El Malecón. Like Fred and Rita's dance in *You'll Never Get Rich*, this type of song is near to, and yet far from, native Cuban music. Although the rhythm may transport us to Havana, the lyric strands us in the U.S.A. Indeed, many latunes don't mention Cuba or Latin America at all. One of the most recorded, "What a Difference a Day Made," has no Latin content other than the rhythm, but this is enough to give the song its foreign air. Latunes speak two languages, one cognitive (the lyric) and the other kinetic (the rhythm). While the rhythm allowed the dancers to partake of the Latin atmosphere, the *ambiente*, the lyric acted as a buffer against the unfamiliarity of the music.

The popularity of Cuban rhythms dates back to the tourist boom of the 1920s. As Americans discovered the island, they discovered its music. The first Cuban song to become a hit in the United States, "The Peanut Vendor," was supposedly discovered by the son of music publisher E. B. Marks while on a honeymoon in Havana. Whether this story is true or not, in February 1931, under the headline "Cuban Invasion," *Time* greeted the arrival of the song about a street vendor who sells peanuts to bored housewives (the sexual innuendo was probably lost in translation). The advance guard of the invasion had reached U.S. shores almost a year earlier, when Don Azpiazu's Havana Casino Orchestra had played "El manisero" (the original of "The Peanut Vendor") at one of New York City's premier vaudeville venues, The Palace. The orchestra, which included the full complement of native instruments, exposed non-Latin New Yorkers, probably for the first time, to Cuban dance music. A couple of days later, a review of the performance commended the young musicians from Havana who had "come up from the South with voodoo and tom-tom motifs in their music and a pair of compelling dances known on the home grounds as the Danzon and the Rumba."[2]

When the sheet music sold a million copies, recording companies and music publishers scrambled to find more tunes, at first sometimes labeled "foxtrot-tangos," to fill the growing demand. (Will Rogers had a unique take on the unexpected success of "The Peanut Vendor": "Nobody can whistle it, that's what makes it the greatest hit of music during our time.")[3] Before the year was out, other Cuban songs were published or recorded—"Adios," "African Lament," "Maria My Own," "Marta (Rambling Rose of the Wildwood)," and even "When Yuba Plays the Rumba on His Tuba," which exemplified the tendency to use the genre for novelty songs. (It is hard to believe that Herman Hupfeld, who thought up the silly song about Yuba down in Cuba with his tuba, also composed "As Time Goes By," and in the same year.) By 1932 the E. B. Marks Music Company listed six hundred Latin American songs in its catalog, and Southern Music Company had started a "Rhumba Sheet Music Club" with the publication of "Green Eyes." The cover art on the sheet music usually portrayed romantic tropical scenes. "Let Me Dream of Havana," a 1936 Mabel Wayne and Marty Symes entry, showed the Morro Castle, framed by a palm tree, under an enormous moon in a starlit sky—a composite possible only in latune-land (fig. 7).

All but forgotten today, two lyricists who played a major part in the rumba rage were Marion Sunshine (1894–1963) and

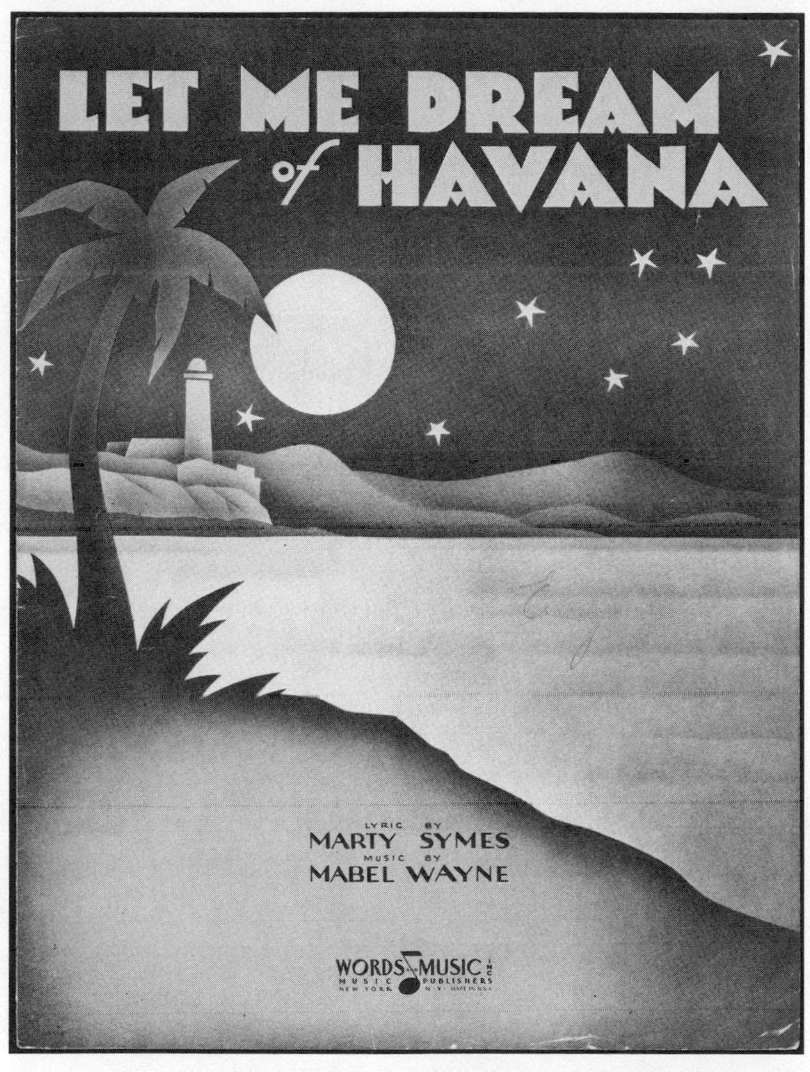

Fig. 7. "Let Me Dream of Havana." Sheet Music, 1936. Lyric by Marty Symes; Music by Mabel Wayne. Copyright 1936 (renewed). Words and Music, Inc., New York, NY. Used by permission.

L. Wolfe Gilbert (1886–1970). Nicknamed "The Rumba Lady," the versatile Sunshine, who started her career in vaudeville as part of the sister act Tempest and Sunshine, married the Cuban bandleader Mario Antobal (brother to the better-known Don Azpiazu) and wrote many of the songs performed by his orchestra, including "They All Look Alike to Pancho," "The Moon over Cuba Was High and So Was I," and "Marianna" (the peanut vendor's daughter). In addition to collaborating with Sunshine on "The Peanut Vendor," Gilbert penned the lyrics to "Marta," "Mama Inez," "Green Eyes," and "María My Own." Not known for his modesty, Gilbert took credit for popularizing the rumba: "The tunes were brought into the country; I saw their potential, wrote American lyrics, and they had their vogue." He was not the only composer to claim the honor: Hoagy Carmichael believed that "One Night in Havana," written after a visit to Cuba in the late 1920s, was "the first American attempt at a rumba with gourds and sticks." (A decade later, fitted with a new lyric, "One Night in Havana" turned into "Chimes of Indiana" and was adopted as one of the two alma maters of Indiana University, which Carmichael had attended.) Burton Lane made the same claim on behalf of "Tony's Wife," a rumba he composed with Harold Adamson, who decades later wrote the words to the *I Love Lucy* theme.[4]

Even though the rumba's popularity induced thousands of Americans to sign up for lessons, the dancing establishment was less than enthusiastic. Already in 1931, after "The Peanut Vendor" had been a hit for only a few months, the American Society of Teachers of Dancing lambasted "the short steps and stomping of the Cuban rumba," calling for "a renaissance of grace." In *Life* an anonymous wag lamented, "Radio bands can kill a tune in six weeks but they don't seem to be able to do anything about that Cuban music." But given the rumba's appeal, dance teachers had no choice but to learn and teach the steps, characterized by a rocking movement of the hips, the so-called Cuban motion, which Arthur Murray confessed had taken him nine years to master. Apparently more of a quick study than Murray, Albert Butler demonstrated the steps of the "dance of the Cuban elite" at the 1935 meeting of New York dance teachers (ironically, the indigenous rumba had emerged from the poorest segments of Cuban society). After a few years, the American Society of Teachers of Dancing had no choice but to acknowledge the inevitable, its president complaining that the rumba had caused the "doom of swing."[5]

While the American rumba derived principally from the *son*, a musical and dance genre popular with the Cuban middle class in the 1920s, some of the sexual suggestiveness of the Afro-Cuban rumba remained in "The Dance of Romance." According to the Reverend R. P. Shuler, a leader of the Methodist Church (and Prohibition Party candidate for senator from California), the fad of the rumba proved that civilization was turning backward to aboriginal lusts and cravings. On a milder note, Arnold Constable's department store advertised an elegant copy of a Lanvin gown called the "Rhumba" with "flowing lines as exciting to fashion as the rhumba is to the dance." Hosiery styles featured tones of gray, wine, and "rhumba." Park Avenue designer Maybelle Manning introduced the "rhumba silhouette," a long, sleek gown with a Spanish train and a ruffled scarf draped across the neck and over the arm. (Manning's clients were surely unaware that the ruffles in *rumbera* costumes were inspired by barnyard fowl, whose mating rituals the rumba simulated.) Even Saks Fifth Avenue jumped on the bandwagon with a panty girdle especially designed "to improve your rhumba" by allowing for free movement while "curbing your curves" (fig. 8).[6]

All over the country rumba bands sprouted, some of them led by Americans passing for Cubans: Alvino Rey (Alvin McBurney), his competitor Alfredo Mendez (Alfred Mendelsohn), and Don Carlos and His Rumba Band (which began its life as Lou Gold and His Orchestra). By contrast, genuine Latin orchestras often resorted to American vocalists to put these songs across. Bob Burke and Chick Bullock (sometimes billed as Chico Bullo—*bulla* is Spanish for noise) sang and recorded with Azpiazu's orchestra, while Rita Hayworth and Dinah Shore did the same with Xavier Cugat, who crowned himself "King of the Rumba." Newspapers ran advertisements for Cuban instruments like "rumba sticks" (claves) and "rumba shakers" (maracas). Nearly every nightclub and cabaret in major cities had a rumba act, including "The Century of Progress" revue at the 1933 Chicago World's Fair. In New York, Latin society bands, such as those led

Fig. 8. "Rhumba Pantie Girdle." Saks Fifth Avenue advertisement. *New York Times,* October 2, 1941. Courtesy Saks Inc.

by Emil Coleman and Enric Madriguera, offered smooth rumbas to downtown cabaret audiences. It was said that there were more rumba bands in Manhattan than in Havana.

Vaudeville revues and Broadway shows quickly picked up on the new dance. The *Cotton Club Revue of 1931* included a number called "La Rhumba," with music by Harold Arlen and lyrics by Ted Koehler. *Bacardi Cocktail,* a 1932 vaudeville revue, starred Don Azpiazu, whose recording of "The Peanut Vendor" helped to launch the Cuban-music fashion. Irving Berlin's rumba "Latins Know How," from *Louisiana Purchase* (1940), provided a musical answer to Helen Lawrenson's infamous *Esquire* article, "Latins Are Lousy Lovers," which asserted that all Cubans know how to do is talk about sex.[7] For the *Goldwyn Follies of 1938,* his last Broadway show, George Gershwin composed "Just Another Rhumba," whose speaker moans that because of the rumba, he can't eat or "slum-bah." *On the Streets of Paris,* a 1939 revue with Abbott and Costello, made Carmen Miranda a star when she rumba'd the "South American way" wearing a fantastic fruit-laden headdress and six-inch heels.

For the mural of the Cuban Pavilion at the 1939 New York World's Fair, the redoubtable Conrado Massaguer drew a rumba band with New York mayor Fiorello LaGuardia playing the maracas and FDR on bass. The spectators included Benito Mussolini, Hermann Göring, the duke of Windsor, Charlie Chaplin, George Bernard Shaw, and Mahatma Gandhi (fig. 9). An example of the irreverent Cuban humor called *choteo,* Massaguer's caricature portrays these famous people entranced by the same rumbera figure he had designed for tourist posters—cleavage, a ruffled skirt with a long slit, open legs. But although the eyes of the world are upon her, the rumbera seems more interested in the makeshift band of American politicians close behind her, for

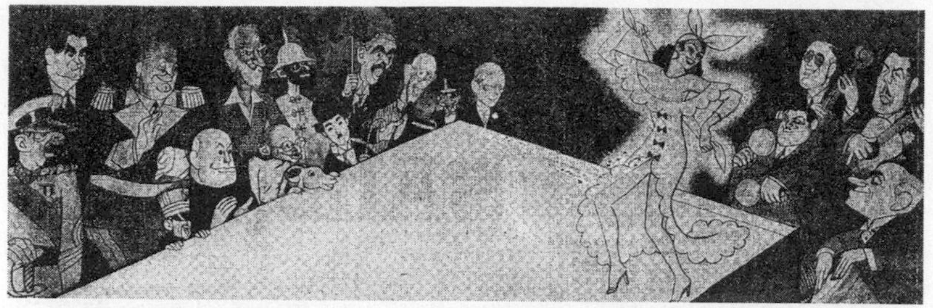

Fig. 9. Cuban Pavilion Mural by Conrado Massaguer, 1939 World's Fair. *New York Times*, June 7, 1939.

whose benefit she wiggles her behind—an equivocal gesture, defiant as well as flirtatious. Perhaps because he had the best view of the rumbera, Mayor LaGuardia liked the caricature, but Cuban authorities had the mural painted over, fearing that Americans might be offended by the picture of FDR ogling a Cuban's ass.

The impact of the rumba on Roosevelt's Good Neighbor Policy was not lost on John Martin, the influential dance critic for the *New York Times*, who argued that the dance could improve relations between Cuba and the United States:

> When we finally get the trick of such an utterly alien manner of moving as that involved in the rumba, we take on with it, willy nilly, a certain amount of Cuban psychology. We simply cannot practice such a movement without producing in ourselves at least a hint of the feeling that prompts the Cuban to move as he does.
>
> We are touching him on his most unrationalized level of experience, where his emotional life begins and many of his motivations unconsciously are formed, and we are transferring something of this elemental state of his mind into our

> own experience at a comparable level. Inevitably we emerge with a closer understanding of him.[8]

What Martin does not mention is that kinetic empathy—sway like them, feel like them—works both ways. If he is right, you cannot move like a Cuban without becoming a little bit *cubano* yourself: Cuban motion breeds Cuban emotions. Once Americans penetrate Cuban psychology, their own emotional makeup will be altered as well (which may explain the smirk on FDR's face as he contemplates the rumbera). Even if Martin exaggerates, his essay—like Massaguer's censored mural—points to the reciprocity of Cuban-American cultural ties. It is well known that during the first half of the twentieth century the United States exerted a powerful influence on Cuban life; less acknowledged is the Cuban footprint on the United States, for the more American Cuba became, the more Cuban America became. And no Cuban product had a greater impact than music. Most Americans never learned to rumba, but in the back of their minds Cuban rhythms, of which the rumba was only the first, were working their metamorphic magic.

This is not to say that these songs, including those imported from Cuba, did not reflect American concerns and values. In Spanish, Lecuona's "Canto Siboney" is a profession of love for Cuba's native inhabitants, the *siboneyes,* who had been extinct for several centuries when Lecuona composed the song. In English, the disappearance of the siboney is even more palpable, for the word no longer refers to a people, but only to "the tune that they croon down Havana way." Although "Canto Siboney" is an art song best suited for an operatic voice, the English-language lyric asserts that "Siboney," a big-band standard for thirty years, is just like other tunes performed by American singers. Not surprisingly, the most popular recording of the song was made by Bing Crosby, the quintessential crooner.

American anxieties about race help to explain why, in English, "Siboney" became self-referential. In "Canto Siboney," a white woman pines for her Indian beloved in no uncertain terms: "Siboney, yo te quiero, yo me muero por tu amor. / Siboney, en tu boca la miel puso su dulzor" (Siboney, I love you, I'm dying for your love. / Siboney, your mouth has the sweetness of honey). It's hard to imagine Margaret Whiting or Helen O'Connell making a similar plea to her dead Apache lover. No matter how closely or distantly the originals were followed, American lyricists took care to remove the racial references that abound in Cuban music. Margarita Lecuona (Ernesto's cousin) is remembered for two compositions with an Afro-Cuban theme: "Babalú," popularized in the United States by Miguelito Valdés and Desi Arnaz (both of whom claimed the title "Mr. Babalú"), and "Tabú," a staple of many Latin orchestras. In "Tabú," the son of a slave gives voice to his desire for an "hembra blanca" (a white female), something which, of course, is "taboo." Recorded by Tony Martin, the English version is sung by a man in love with a woman who is taboo because he is married to someone else. But if falling in love with another woman were really taboo, songwriters would be out of business. Once again, what is truly taboo is the theme of interracial romance. As if to reinforce the racial cleansing, Dinah Shore answered Tony Martin with another rumba on the same topic, "Is It Taboo (to Fall in Love with You)?"

In the original of "Mama Inez," the speaker is a *negrito,* a black boy, who tells Mamá Inés that he is going dancing with "todos los negros" (all the blacks). The English version, popularized by Maurice Chevalier, whites out the negrito, putting in his place Chevalier and his gallicized English. Mamá Inés, the boy's *madrina*, or godmother, turns into "mon Inez," a rumba dancer. The refrain in Spanish—"Ay Mamá Inés, todos los negros tomamos café" (Hey Mama Inez, all of us blacks drink coffee) —changes to: "Oh mon Inez, no Cuban rum's like the rum-ba for me." Like "Siboney," Mama Inez becomes a song about itself, the "brand-new fandango."

Other examples of whitening: just as Marion Sunshine turns "La negra Quirina" (Black Quirina) into "The Cuban Belle," another prolific latune-smith, Marjorie Harper, renders "Negra consentida" (Spoiled Black Woman) as "My Pet Brunette"—a translation that retains the idea of the cherished beloved but changes skin color into hair color. Three other Ernesto Lecuona classics endured a similar bleaching: "Danza lucumí," inspired by African ritual dances, turned into "From One Love to Another"; "La comparsa," which evokes the sound of a black carnival celebration, became "For Want of a Star," a lachrymose ballad about a man who has lost his sweetheart; "Canto indio" became "Dust on the Moon." (To judge by the last two titles, Lecuona's melodies exerted a curious astronomical influence on American lyricists.)

The irony, of course, is that the erasure of race is all but undone by the musical setting. When Tony Martin sings "Taboo," the arrangement incorporates a flute line and muted drums that imitate jungle sounds, though there is nothing in the speaker's banal predicament to motivate them. This dissonance is even more pronounced in recordings that incorporate fragments of the Spanish lyric, as was often the custom, for then the whiting-out in the new lyric clashes with the race-based Spanish words. But since English is the only cognitive language, nobody notices. Like the term *siboney*, Spanish functions as ambient sound, a component of atmosphere that lacks communicative value. The voices of men and women of color are heard only in the instruments, not in articulate speech.

To be fair, race was not the only determinant in these transpositions. For one thing, since American lyricists often had only a faint idea what the original was about, they were guided by metrical requirements rather than subject matter. And even when the lyricists knew the original, they were bound by the accentual pattern and syllabic count of the melody. If meter and meaning clashed, meaning gave way. Nothing in Mexican María Grever's bolero "Muñequita linda" (Pretty little doll), explains its translation as "Magic Is the Moonlight," except that both phrases have six syllables in duple meter. The stimulus for refashioning "Muñequita linda" as "Magic Is the Moonlight" may have been nothing more than the initial alliteration, which the American lyricist, Charles Pasquale, exploited to good effect. Were it not for atmospherics—the bolero rhythm—the listener would not suspect that "Magic Is the Moonlight" is a latune.

Mitchell Parish, who wrote the lyrics to both "Sidewalks of Cuba" and "Star Dust," remarked that when putting words to Latin songs he did not let himself be governed by any "foreign idea."[9] As a result, at times the English words to Latin songs are almost dummy lyrics, provisional words that a lyricist contrives to get a feel for the meter and that often are little more than gibberish (though in one famous instance, "Tea for Two," the dummy lyric ended up as the definitive one). When Al Stillman renders the refrain of "Piel canela" (Cinnamon skin), "Me importas tú y tú y tú / y nadie más que tú" (I like you and you and you / and no one else but you) as "A new-born rose, a-ding, a-dong. / How beautiful it grows, a-ding, a-dong" ("A-Ding, A-Dong"), the prosodic requirements produce something like a Dadaist poem or nursery rhyme. (Perhaps unsatisfied with this effort, Stillman wrote another set of lyrics to the song, "Until Tonight," that does without dings and dongs.)

Capó's bolero-mambo also yielded "You Too, You Too," recorded by the Andrews Sisters, which does a better job of translating the Spanish-language refrain: "I like romance—you too, you too. / I wanna take a chance—you too, you too." But in this case also the racial coloration of a song about a girl with "cinnamon skin" induces the lyricist (Marian Banks) to turn "Piel canela" into another self-referential latune:

> There's a melody that's called "Piel canela,"
> very popular beneath the Cuban moon.
> When they sip their substitute for sarsaparilla,
> how the Cubans love to listen to that tune.
> Everybody's dancing to "Piel canela,"
> it's the favorite in the juke at Sloppy Joe's.
> It was sung to me beneath a beach umbrella
> so I'm qualified to tell you how it goes—

Give Marian Banks credit for rhyming "piel canela" with "sarsaparilla" and "beach umbrella," but not for the implication that "Piel canela" was a Cuban import. Although the song was a hit in Cuba, as in much of Latin America, Bobby Capó was Puerto Rican. Nonetheless, since back-of-the-mind Cuba often stands for Latin America as a whole, the locale of the song, if not its location, is accurate. (One thing I have not been able to figure out, however, is what would be the Cuban substitute for sarsaparilla.)

The frequent erasure of the differences among Latin American nations is especially pronounced in the numerous geographical latunes, which purported to familiarize Americans with foreign locations: "Ah-bah-nah, Coo-bah," "Managua, Nicaragua," "It Happened in Monterrey," "It Began in Yucatan," "In Santiago, Chile (Tain't Chilly at All)," "You Can't Say No in Acapulco,"

"You Can in Yucatan." No matter where the music takes you, the orchestra is playing a rumba. That is why it isn't chilly in Chile: because the hot beat conjures up the latune-land's tropical climate.

(A quick survey of the lay of the land: a tropical island—or, for ease of rhyme, a tropic isle—where palm trees sway in the breeze and waves lap against the shore to the swish-swish of maracas. When you bask in the sun of this beguiling isle, instead of a tan you develop a Latin glow. When you walk in the moonlight, you are bathed in the aroma of perfume and sighs. Although vegetation abounds, a few species thrive: peanuts, bananas, coconuts. The female inhabitants of latune-land are all señoritas; the males all caballeros—often gay but never unmanly. Some of the local lovelies include Chiquita Banana—a.k.a. the First Lady of Fruit—the improbably named Tangerine—unlike Chiquita, not a fruit but a girl—Rita the Rumba Queen, Cleo from Rio, and Conchita Marquita Lolita Pepita Rosita Juanita Lopez, or "the rose of Juarez" for short. Among the male population you will find Cuban Pete, South American Joe, José O'Neill—the Cuban heel—a few Latins from Manhattan and the Broadway Caballero. Where is this place? According to Cole Porter, it's in Panama, which he rhymes with Shangri-la ["Visit Panama"]. According to Mack Gordon, who boasted that he developed his flair for Latin music by smoking Cuban cigars, it's in Acapulco, otherwise known as Paradise ["In Acapulco"].)

Like other latunes, rumbas have often been denigrated as watered-down or flaccid Cuban music. But their ersatz quality doesn't bother me, because it doesn't bother them. Rumbas make no pretense of being anything other than bowdlerized Cubanism. Even the natives of latune-land are not always what they seem: the Tangerine of Johnny Mercer's song fools everyone into thinking she's a dark-eyed Argentine with makeup bought at Macy's. The real name of the original "Latin from Manhattan" is Suzy Donahue. "Channa from Havana" is Channa Cohen from Brooklyn. And Jose O'Neill started out as "a second grader from Decatur." Were these characters authentically Cuban (whatever "authentic" may mean in such a mongrel culture as Cuba's), the listener would not be able to identify with them to the same extent. We like them because, like the millions of Americans who bought rumba records and attended rumba parties, they only play at being Latin.

Irving Berlin's "On a Roof in Manhattan," from *Face the Music* (1932), summarized the latune lover's aspirations as building a castle in Spain on a roof in Manhattan so that the two lovers can "pretend to be Latin." You can ask what castles in Spain have to do with Latins in Manhattan. Next to nothing is the answer, though in the lofty domain of latune-land the question is irrelevant. Castles in Spain are nothing but thin air. Atmosphere is also air, as is music. However counterfeit, Latins from Manhattan point to the fundamental achievement of latunes: the coupling of English words and Cuban rhythms, a marriage made in Havana heaven. The ordinary or trifling subject matter aside, there is always something delightful, a pleasant culture shock (skeptics might say, schlock), in an American rumba. The hidden melody of the words, the music of the English language, finds an unexpected home in the company of maracas, claves, and bongos. Enveloped in a Latin atmosphere—and nothing creates atmosphere like music—English acquires a lightness, a lift, that Berlin images as a lofty domain. If the lyrics relieve the strangeness of the rhythm, the rhythm gives the words wings. Even when—or maybe especially when—the coupling engenders outlandish rhymes like "sarsaparilla" and "piel canela."

THREE

Music for the Eyes

The earliest images of Cuba in American film are grainy clips taken during the Spanish-American War. In the years that followed, during the silent era, the war continued to dominate in such films as *A Message to García* (1916), *Shame* (1917), and *The Rough Riders* (1927). One of the most popular, *The Bright Shawl* (1923), based on a novel by Joseph Hergesheimer, uses the Cuban struggle for independence as background for a love story about a wealthy young American who falls for a Spanish dancer. It was not until the advent of talkies, and particularly of musicals, that the image of Cuba as a romantic paradise began to appear regularly on the Hollywood screen. Starting in the early thirties and for the next three decades, countless movies would include Cuban material. Often it was no more than a mention of someone going to or returning from Havana; at other times, scenes or whole movies were set in Cuba, and a few were filmed there. And when the locale wasn't Cuban, the atmosphere often was.

In *Luxury Liner* (1948), teen-aged Jane Powell is an aspiring soprano who intends to sing a selection from *Aida* for the ship's passengers. Playing himself, an irascible Xavier Cugat huffs at Powell: "I don't care what *you're* planning to sing. *I'm* playing 'The Peanut Vendor.'" It's not as if Cugie has his destination in mind, for the ship is heading to Rio de Janeiro. (Powell ends up singing "The Peanut Vendor"—but as an operatic aria.) From Ginger Rogers and Fred Astaire's "La Carioca" (a rumba) in *Flying Down to Rio* (1933) to the steamy night-club scene in *Guys and Dolls* (1955) during which Marlon Brando does a mambo, Cuban rhythms pervaded Hollywood musicals, often with little regard for geography or verisimilitude. In *Six Lessons from Madame La Zonga* (1941), remembered today—mostly by me—for its title song, a cowboy band predictably named the Rough Riders goes to Havana, where, with the help of Madame La Zonga (Lupe Velez), its members trade their lariats for maracas. The reason the band changes its tune: "Everything is rumba." As late as Elvis Presley's *Fun in Acapulco* (1963), thirty years after Americans first attempted Cuban motion, Elvis sings "No Room to Rumba in a Sports Car" as he zips along the streets of the Mexican resort.

The first musical in Twentieth-Century Fox's Latin American cycle was the enormously successful *Down Argentine Way* (1940), whose title song is not a tango, as one would expect, but a rumba.

In an unintentionally humorous moment, someone remarks that Argentina is the place "for a really hot conga." But not any hotter than Brazil, as *My Sister Eileen* (1955) demonstrates when Janet Leigh leads Brazilian naval cadets in a conga in, of all places, Greenwich Village. *The Trumpet Blows* (1934) stars George Raft and Adolphe Menjou as Mexican bandits who roam the countryside to the strains of "My Heart Does the Rumba." *Blondie Goes Latin* (1941), based on the comic strip, culminates in a "Brazilian Cotillion" that begins as a rumba and ends with a conga (to which Blondie tap-dances). In *Panama Hattie* (1942), Lena Horne does "The Sping," "a Cubaninic, Harleminic, Caribbinic, Castilinic thing" (the name agglutinates "Spanish" and "Swing," or perhaps "Spic" and "Swing"). In *Copacabana* (1947), set in the New York nightclub, Andy Russell warbles with more rhyme than reason that his heart was doing a bolero in the middle of Rio de Janeiro. No less improbably, *My Friend Irma Goes West* (1950) has Dean Martin crooning "Querida mía" while he dances a smooth rumba out in cactus country.

In the 1930s and 1940s, Roosevelt's Good Neighbor Policy undoubtedly gave Latin-themed numbers and musicals a boost. But as MGM producer Arthur Freed pointed out, what made these pictures was the "rumba stuff." Whether it was springtime in the Rockies or carnival in Costa Rica, the ambient sounds were Cuban, with an occasional tango or samba thrown in. And as if the rumba stuff weren't enough, for twenty years the person in charge of vetting the Latin American content of Hollywood films for the Production Code Association was the former head of the Cuban Tourist Commission in New York, Havana-born and -bred Addison Durland. If all of the places in maraca musicals seem to be replicas of latune-land, that same "ridiculous tropical country," as one Latin American critic complained, Durland deserves part of the credit. He was meticulous in his cubano-centrism. Although he saw nothing wrong with rumbas in Rio or boleros in Buenos Aires, he asked that the word "papaya" be excised from *Law of the Tropics* (1941) because in some parts of Cuba (though not in the rest of Latin America) the word is slang for female genitalia.[1]

Luxury Liner was not the first movie in which "The Peanut Vendor" was heard, nor was Madame La Zonga the only Cuban character played by Lupe Velez, the Mexican Spitfire. Both occurred a decade earlier in *The Cuban Love Song* (1931), one of the first talkies set in Cuba, in which Lupe plays Nenita Lopez, the peanut vendor herself, who falls in love with a handsome American marine. In spite of the title and the story line, however, *The Cuban Love Song* is not escapist fare. As the opening credits roll, the first tune we hear is not "The Peanut Vendor" but the "Marines' Hymn," which accompanies background shots of an American battleship cutting the waves. The two songs will establish a counterpoint between two ideas of Cuba: as theater of war and as tourist destination. This counterpoint will express the movie's theme: the interplay between American might and Latin seductiveness.

In February 1917, marine Terry Burke (Lawrence Tibbett, a fine tenor who had a lackluster Hollywood career) is sent to Cuba along with the rest of his troop. The shores of Tripoli become the Havana harbor as their battleship steams past the Morro Castle, with the camera drawing the viewer's attention to the contrast between the ancient Spanish cannons and the battleship's sleek guns. Motoring around Havana like the drunken sailor that he is, Terry rear-ends Nenita's donkey cart. At the police station, Nenita accuses him of ruining her peanut business, but the marines arrive just in time to save Terry from jail. Enamored of the childlike Nenita (the name means "little baby"), Terry woos her, and she finally yields. But World War I interrupts their idyll. In a scene that seems lifted from a Tarzan movie, Terry's buddies paddle up a jungle river to retrieve their friend, who is cavorting with Nenita in the countryside.

Flash forward to 1930. Badly wounded in the European war (think Jake Barnes), Terry never went back to Cuba, as he had promised Nenita. Instead, he married his former fiancée, Crystal, a rich New Yorker. Celebrating their tenth wedding anniversary in a nightclub, the childless couple hears a new song that is sweeping the nation: "The Peanut Vendor." His memories of Cuba reawakened, Terry rushes out of the nightclub and goes to the docks, where the ghost of his young self materializes, singing "The Peanut Vendor" in full marine regalia. Ghostly Terry pleads with his flesh-and-blood counterpart to return to Cuba: "Terry, that little island is still there—Cuba, there's magic in the name alone. She's dancing, she's laughing at you." In the next scene, we see Terry once again on a ship that's going past the Morro Castle, but this time he is dressed like a tourist.

After several days of fruitless search, Terry finds out that in his absence Nenita—a tropical Butterfly—passed away. Walking back from her grave, he hears "The Cuban Love Song" in a voice like Nenita's—but it's not another ghost. On the back of a donkey cart, a boy with dark curly hair is singing the song that his mother taught him. It's his son. Terry and Terry Jr. return to New York, where Terry's wife graciously welcomes the offspring of her husband's Cuban adventure into the family.

The Cuba of *The Cuban Love Song* is not the country of the 1920s tourist boom but that of the American occupations. In the early months of 1917, when the movie begins, American troops did indeed land in Cuba to quell an uprising by disaffected politicians (Cubans call it the February Revolution). So far, the movie reflects Cuban history accurately. But other details distort the picture. For one thing, if Nenita, as her son insinuates, died in the flu epidemic of 1918, he would not have been old enough to learn "El manisero" from her. For another, although Terry hears this song in 1917, it was not composed by Moisés Simons until ten years later. The most glaring anachronism, however, has to do with Cuba itself. When Terry goes back in 1930, he remarks that "Everything's exactly as it used to be"—Cubans still get around in donkey-carts; peanut vendors peddle their merchandise as they did before; the policemen haven't aged a day. Yet the

Havana of 1930 was far different than the Havana of 1917, for in the intervening years the city had been transformed by rapid growth and modernization. When Terry Sr. remarks to his boy on the cart that he speaks English like an American, Terry Jr. responds, "I am American. My father is a big soldier over there." The belated echo of George M. Cohan's march suggests that the movie is stuck in a time warp. Even if in 1930 Terry arrives on a cruise ship rather than a battleship, Cuba remains the struggling nation that it had been during the first two decades of the century.

The denouement explains these distortions. Orphaned Terry Jr.—half Cuban, half American—is Cuba after the Spanish-American War, a fledgling republic in need of tutelage by the United States (this was the main rationale for the Platt Amendment). In this respect, the movie is a transparent allegory of paternalism, if not of annexation. Less easy to construe, however, is what Terry Jr.'s adoption does for his American parents. When father and son are riding in the back of the cart, Terry Jr. pulls out some peanuts from his pocket, throws one into the air, and catches it in his mouth. He asks his father whether he can accomplish the same trick. He tries but misses. "I guess I can't do it anymore," Terry laughs, in a thinly veiled allusion to his condition. Terry can shrug off his impotence only because he has found Terry Jr., a younger, intact version of himself.

Of course, the idea that the United States needed Cuba to complete itself had been around for more than a hundred years.

But when Thomas Jefferson singled out the island as the most valuable acquisition the Union could make, he was thinking of strategic advantages that, by 1930, had become largely irrelevant, since the United States already had a naval base in Guantánamo and the Panama Canal. Instead, *The Cuban Love Song* suggests that the impulse to annex Cuba arises from a disability or impairment internal to America, as if this country, for all of its might, were incapable of perpetuating itself without an infusion of Cuban (or, more acceptably, half-Cuban) blood. Terry Jr.'s "annexation" indicates that America's interest in things Cuban was not only a fad; or rather, that the fad gave voice to muted needs and anxieties. Initially the symbol of American strength, Terry ends up as an example of American weakness. "I'll never be any good again," he says to Crystal after the war.

Even though *The Cuban Love Song* was a box-office hit, several years passed before the next musical with a Cuban theme. By the time *Rumba* was released in 1935, thoughts of possession of the island had receded, in part because of the Great Depression, in part because of the abrogation of the Platt Amendment. The marines have left; the tourists have arrived—and with them gangsters, hangers-on, and other shady characters. Among the latter is Joe Martin (George Raft), a dancer who goes to Cuba fleeing the mob. In Cuba he falls for a spoiled, wealthy Manhattanite, Di Harrison (Carole Lombard), whose yacht is anchored off the Morro Castle (and seems almost as big). After Di dumps him, Joe follows her to New York. When she learns that the mob is planning to shoot him in the middle of his rumba act, she rushes to his side. As the rapt audience wonders whether the dance of romance will turn into a *danse macabre*, Di and Joe rumba once again, the way they had in Havana. But no one gets shot, since the murder plot was a publicity stunt dreamed up by Joe's manager. "Best one I ever thought up," he says. "Put you over with a bang."

Designed to capitalize on the success of *Bolero* (1935), in which Raft played a tango dancer, *Rumba* reunited Raft and Lombard, neither of whom looks comfortable in Cuban motion. Raft struts around lethargically, like a drugged peacock, while Lombard assumes languid poses vaguely timed to the endlessly repeated "Rhythm of the Rumba," another of those self-referential latunes whose entire lyric consists of one sentence: "It's the rhythm of the rumba." With a sneer for every occasion and a vocabulary limited to "dough" and "dame," Joe Martin sounds less like a Latin Lover than like Little Caesar. His excuse is that he is only "half Cuban"; he was born in New York and doesn't speak a word of Spanish (yet his name, bizarrely, echoes that of the Cuban patriot José Martí). Nevertheless, Di regards him as the genuine Cuban article: "What difference does it make where he comes from?" The rumba makes the man.

Even though the hackneyed story about the street-smart dancer and the slumming socialite could have been set anywhere, *Rumba* does not skimp on local color. But the question, as always, is how local the color really is. Often, it is rather "locale" color, a tissue of clichés. As the movie opens, numbers dance in the air, and the camera pans over sheet after sheet of lottery tickets. Havana is in the grip of gambling fever, the natives frantic with expectation. Playing a hunch, Joe buys a ticket and wins. When he goes to collect, he finds out that his ticket is counterfeit. A few scenes later, musical numbers replace lottery numbers, and the difference between the authentic and the counterfeit becomes harder to spot. In a little town in the countryside, Joe discovers the "rumba," portrayed as a fantastic hybrid of the native rumba and the American ballroom dance. In New York, Joe applies what he learned in Cuba to star in a musical revue whose showstopper is "The Birth of the Rumba," a history of the dance from its origins to the present.

The curtain rises on a night in the tropics, with swaying palms and jungle sounds. Bare-chested black men, their legs in irons, file in from the wings, shuffling their feet to the beat of maracas and bongos, as if the steps of the rumba originated in the constrained movements of men in chains (it did not). Earlier in the movie, Joe's agent had tricked a Texas cattleman into backing Joe's nightclub by assuring him that the money would be used to assemble "the most beautiful bunch of calves in all the world." Of course, the agent is thinking not of calves of cattle but of the calves of the *ur*-rumberos, human cattle. As the stage brightens, the shadowy procession of black men vanishes. In its place, couples dressed in Spanish-style outfits dance to "The Rhythm of the Rumba." None of the dancers is black. The final whitening touch occurs when blonde Di fills in for Joe's regular partner, Carmelita, whose name literally means "Brown." (In Hispanic Hollywood, "Carmelita" was a favorite name: the Mexican Spitfire was Carmelita, as was the prize thoroughbred in *Down Argentine Way*.)

Although the origins of the rumba do go back to preemancipation Cuba, the replacement of the Negro slaves by the Spanish dancers effaces the centuries of racial mixing, human and cultural, that made Cuba and its music what they are. But in the 1930s miscegenation was not a topic that Hollywood wanted to broach; it was "Tabú." And so, like some of the latunes discussed in the last chapter, "The Birth of the Rumba" depicts the evolution of this music as a progression into the light in both the atmospheric and racial senses.

An equally blatant bleaching occurs in "She's a Latin from Manhattan," the campy production number from *Go into Your Dance* (1935), released within a few months of *Rumba*. As a globe of the world turns, the camera zooms in on Spain, where Dolores "does the rumba for us" while Al Jolson belts out the song. Next thing, Dolores is dancing on top of the globe: the rumba has conquered the world. But nowhere is there an inkling of the music's mixed blood. Even Cuba is not in the picture, having been replaced by Spain. And Dolores is really Suzy Donahue, a Broadway chorus girl. Amazingly, in the next scene Jolson performs the title song, "Go into Your Dance," in blackface.

In *Rumba* and *The Cuban Love Song*, music shares the stage with melodrama. This would no longer happen in the maraca musicals of the 1940s, which relied only on what Bosley Crowther, the *New York Times* movie critic, called "that Latin quelque-chose."[2] In these movies, the plot subserves the atmosphere, and since the atmosphere is gay, the plots are silly. Maraca musicals use one of two simple story lines: either Americans go to Latin America, or Latins come to the United States. In the first instance, the Americans bathe in the Latin glow and return to their native environment, their lives changed by the exposure. In the other story line, the atmosphere drifts north, normally in the person of an entertainer—Xavier Cugat, Carmen Miranda, Lupe Velez, Cesar Romero—who turns an American location into a Latin locale.

As the third installment in Fox's maraca tetralogy, *Week-End in Havana* (1941) makes no secret that it is a cinematic travelogue about "Hollywood's best good neighbor."[3] Nan Spencer (Alice Faye), a Macy's salesgirl, has been saving for years to take a holiday in Havana. When her cruise ship, *The Cuban Queen*, runs aground off the coast of Florida, she refuses to sign the waiver of liability until she has enjoyed the fun-filled vacation—"a treasure of pleasure"—promised by the company's brochure. Worried about a lawsuit, the company's owner dispatches his future son-in-law, Jay Williams (John Payne), to make sure that Nan's holiday lives up to expectations. Although Jay flops as a companion, he hires a local Cuban-about-town, Monte Blanca (Cesar Romero), to entertain Nan with romance and rumba. The complications begin when Monte's girlfriend (Carmen Miranda) gets wind that Monte has been dallying with sweet Nan. After switching partners a few times, Nan and Jay finally realize that they love each other—an effect of "Tropical Magic," the movie's hit ballad written by Mack Gordon and Harry Warren, Fox's latune specialists.

Retitled *A La Habana Me Voy* (I'm going to Havana), the film was spectacularly premiered in Cuba's capital with Cesar Romero's cousins and the vice president of Cuba in attendance. Significantly, the premiere was sponsored by the Cuban Tourist Commission. Although the movie didn't draw large audiences (then as now, Latin Americans prefer American movies about America), its publicity value was recognized by all. More than any of the other Fox musicals, *Week-End in Havana* was inspired by the tourism industry, probably because Havana, unlike Rio or Buenos Aires, was a prime tourist destination. (As part of its promotional campaign, Fox held contests in various cities; the winners received a free weekend in Havana.) Of the four movies in its Latin American cycle (the others are *Down Argentine Way*, *That Night in Rio*, and *The Gang's All Here*), *Week-End in Havana* is the only one whose protagonist plays the part of a tourist; and it is surely not accidental that the movie was released in October, just in time for the winter season (unexpectedly interrupted two months later by the Japanese attack on Pearl Harbor).

Flaunting its status as tourist bait, the movie opens with snow falling over Manhattan. The scene then shifts to a shop window that advertises cruises to Cuba, "Holiday Isle of the Tropics." As snow piles up on the sidewalk, the mannequins in the window start moving to the beat of a conga drum. After a few seconds, a Carmen Miranda doll springs to life to ask the musical question, "How would you like to spend a weekend in Havana?" Who wouldn't? The display is the movie itself, a window to the warm and splendid Pearl of the Antilles. Nineteenth-century travelers used to remark on the openness of Cuban houses, whose large, curtainless windows facing the street made it easy for passersby to examine their interiors and inhabitants. The movie's opening makes the same point. Havana is a showcase, a window anyone can look into, even a hosiery salesgirl. A few minutes after the opening scenes, a fluid montage of Technicolor shots of the Morro Castle, El Malecón, Sloppy Joe's, and other Havana landmarks (not excluding the naked nymphs of the Gran Casino Nacional fountain) pass before the viewer's eyes, while "Siboney" and "Mama Inez" play in the background. To make the point even more obvious, Jay reads to Nan from a guidebook, perhaps Consuelo Hermer and Marjorie May's *Havana Mañana*, which appeared in the same year as the movie.

A question about the window display: When Carmen and her band start to play, where are they? In the movie, she is Rosita Rivas, a famous Cuban entertainer who sings (in Portuguese) in a Havana nightspot (called the Casino Madrileño). But in the shop window she is only Carmen Miranda, backed as usual by the Banda da Lua; and she is not in Havana (or in New York for that matter). The plain backdrop of white arches—the gateway to dreams—against a blue sea emphasizes the abstractness of the setting. Before Carmen appears, we first hear and see the conga drum, followed by the bongos, the maracas, and the clave—and immediately we know where we are: in lala-tune-land.

The last installment in Fox's maraca quartet, *The Gang's All Here* (1943), raises the issue of place even more pointedly: Where is the "here" in the title? On its make-believe holiday, the gang has taken a northward path: starting from Buenos Aires (*Down Argentine Way*), it proceeded to Rio (*That Night in Rio*), and from there to Havana. Where did the gang go after the weekend in Havana? Like its predecessors, *The Gang's All Here* opens with a musical number that establishes the atmosphere; in this case, it's a close-up of a young man singing "Brazil" against a pitch-black background that renders him invisible but for his head. As he sings in Portuguese, the camera pans to the left, revealing the bow of a ship named the *S.S. Brazil.* The singing head is actually a figurehead; and "here" is Brazil, but it's a ship, not a country. As passengers begin streaming down the gangway—a visual pun: the gangway is how the gang disembarks—the skyline comes into view, finally settling the question implicit in the title: "here" is New York City.

Or is it? In addition to sacks of sugar and coffee, the ship's cargo includes a stash of tropical fruits in the shape of a pyramid—Carmen Miranda's hat, under which sits Carmen Miranda's head. (Busby Berkeley, who directed the movie, had a strange attachment to detached body parts.) A car arrives bearing a representative of Mayor La Guardia, who gives Carmen the key to the city. When the camera moves to a long shot of the pier, viewers realize that they have been tricked again, for the scene is taking place on a nightclub stage. The only crew on this voyage is the stage crew. Brazil is not Brazil and New York is not New York—or only the make-believe New York of stage sets, which stands in for the real New York of the nightclub's audience, which, in turn, stands in for the audience of moviegoers.

To explain the intricate trompe l'oeil, Carmen Miranda breaks into song: although you may be hearing a tropical drum and drinking tropical rum, you're not in a tropical spot. And although the "atmosphere" may make your heart flutter, it's enough to reach for the bread and butter to discover that you're in New York. The lyric of "You Discover You're in New York" summarizes the philosophy that Jay Williams, a hard-nosed Yankee, espoused in *Week-End in Havana.* A Latin atmosphere may nourish the heart, but it doesn't put food on the table. For a reality check, reach for the bread and butter. (To which Cesar Romero would have replied: "Ah, señor, but man does not live by bread alone.") The opening sequence of *The Gang's All Here* unmasks the illusion that makes maraca musicals possible, even as it foists that illusion on its audience one more time. So where is the "here" in the title? Where are the singing heads? Where are the shop-window musicians of *Week-End in Havana?* Wherever a movie is tricking moviegoers into believing that they are somewhere else, in the lofty domain of Cuban/Latin locales.

Although Cesar Romero gets only fourth billing in *Week-End in Havana*, he dominates the movie, not an easy thing to do when Carmen Miranda is also in the cast. But Romero keeps our eyes fixed on him. Antic and romantic by turns, no sooner is he leading Faye in a rumba than he is being chased around the casino by a furious Miranda. Even more than Carmen, Cesar incarnates the spirit of fun, of communal mirth-making, that distinguishes *Week-End in Havana* and other maraca musicals. He is the glue in the gang, the character around which the other characters coalesce. Wherever the action is—gambling and otherwise—there is Monte, wearing more hats than Miranda: he is Nan's love interest, Rosita's love interest, Jay's employee and rival, the mark of the shady casino owner, and the luckiest man in Havana, who makes a fortune at roulette without even trying (and then throws it all away).[4]

Nattily dressed in an off-white dinner jacket, Monte enters the scene when Nan sings "Tropical Magic," like the genie sprung from the Bacardi bottle. A bit later, dancing with Monte, Nan becomes aware of the change he has wrought in her. The resident expert in romance and rumba, Monte turns wilting wallflowers into social butterflies. His gift to Nan, as to the gang as a whole, is a heightened feeling of community. In the last scene of the movie, when Monte is trying to escape his pursuers, he saves himself not by making good on his debt—Jay refuses to lend him the money—but by blending into the crowd doing "The Ñango," another of those faux Cuban dances that abound in maraca musicals (other examples: the panamania, the rhumboogie, the sarumba), and that always involve large groups of dancers. Losing himself in the whirling throng, Monte returns to his element. Why the *ñango* (a made-up word)? Because it's the name for what animates the gang, "simply wild about the ñango." Call it *ñango*, or call it *bilongo*, Monte has it.

For contrast, think of the Hollywood Western, a genre whose heyday coincided with that of maraca musicals. If Westerns glorify the individual, the simple, genuine self against the world, to borrow a phrase from Emerson, maraca musicals give voice to sociability, to the merged self or communal ego. Instead of duels, duets. Instead of posses, conga lines. Instead of ghost towns, Havana. In the American imagination, the West and Cuba stand for a place apart, for a kind of frontier, but that's where the resemblance ends. There are no "Weekends in Yuma" or "Holidays in Tombstone." The West is the big country that tests a man's mettle, whether he is running away or settling down. Cuba is the little island where men and women go not to run away but to get away, an escape from ordinary life that involves a merging into community rather than a detachment from it. Bilongo is a species of belonging.

In *America in the Movies,* Michael Wood discusses what he calls "the American myth of a Fall into social life," that is, the belief that once the individual—almost always a man—joins a community, he loses his selfhood.[5] Maraca musicals, perhaps like musicals generally, send the opposite message. It is in the midst of community, in the feeling of shared experience whose quintessential expression is the dance, that people discover who they really are. It's not a Fall, it's a Redemption. Awkward as he looks, Jay finds his true self doing the ñango rather than going over the company books. And he has Monte to thank. The strict opposite of the strong, silent type of Westerns, Monte the mountebank is the hero of a world that celebrates touch, discourse, human contact, a world where even the stars, as he says, are "dancing rumbas in the sky."

The identification of Latinness with community surely helps to explain the proliferation of congas in maraca and other musicals. The conga line, in which the dancers are physically linked to one another, served as a visually appealing metaphor of Latin-tinged connectedness. In *Strike Up the Band* (1940), a Mickey Rooney–Judy Garland vehicle, Busby Berkeley stages a seven-minute conga remarkable for the number of ways in which he forms, unforms, and reforms the rows of dancers that snake across a high-school auditorium. Imported from Cuba in the late 1930s, the conga was inclusive, as a community should be, for anyone could learn the simple steps. "Kindergarten Conga," the only mildly catchy number in the otherwise dreadful score of *Moon over Miami* (1941), makes the point that even kindergartners can do it. The title of another 1941 composition corroborates the ease with which this dance can be mastered: "I Came, I Saw, I Conga'd." A partial list of the Hollywood conga roll: "Doing the Conga" from *Down Argentine Way* (1940); "Cali-Conga" from *A Night at Earl Carroll's* (1940); "Congeroo" and "Conga Beso" from *Hellzapopin'* (1941); "Doing the Conga" from *Up in the Air* (1941); "Ora O Conga," a lusophone entry, from *Rio Rita* (1942); "Boogie Woogie Conga" from *Four Jacks and a Jill* (1942); "Conga from Honga" from *The Fleet's In* (1942); "I Hate the Conga" from *Born to Sing* (1942); and *La Conga Nights* (1940), about a "music moron" who opens a nightclub in New York.

Although intended only as a "programmer"—that is, as the lesser half of a double bill—*Cuban Pete* (1946) offers a typical illustration of the other type of maraca musical, the one that resorts to the "Latin-to-Manhattan" story line. With a running time of little over an hour, *Cuban Pete* lacks the production values and intricate plotting of *Week-End in Havana.* It has no spectacular dances or big-name actors. Except for the stock footage of Havana and a plantation scene, the movie unfolds on a few rudimentary sets: an office complex, various rooms, and—most important—a nightclub stage. The male lead is Desi Arnaz, at the time known principally as a band leader, who plays himself. Opposite him is Joan Fulton, a pretty blonde who appeared in many movies throughout the 1940s and 1950s (perhaps her best-remembered role is Sweet Sue in *Some Like It Hot*). In his autobiography, Arnaz rates *Cuban Pete* "a B-minus picture" whose principal value was to drum up business for his band, which apparently it did.

Arnaz had made his Hollywood debut in *Too Many Girls* (1940), in which he played Manuelito Lynch, a young man from Argentina who is a football prodigy as well as a conga-drumming demon. The climactic scene in the movie shows what can happen when a Latin is let loose in Middle America. After the big victory, Manuelito leads his classmates into a large plaza where a bonfire burns. With the flames spiraling around him, he begins to pound on his drum and make strange noises. Picking up the chant, the students form conga lines. Some carry torches, others the *farolas* (lanterns) of carnival celebrations. The scene cuts to a lab where a professor is peering through his microscope: the paramecia on the slide are also bumping and grinding to the conga beat—an example of the hypnotic spell of the music, which entrances even the lowest forms of life. As the movie ends, Desi is engulfed in flames, while the screen becomes a blur of screaming, swirling bodies.

Although Arnaz received good notices for *Too Many Girls*, during the next few years he got only small, mostly nonsinging roles in such forgettable movies as *Father Takes a Wife* (1941), *Four Jacks and a Jill* (1941), *The Navy Comes Through* (1942), and *Bataan* (1943). After the war, he was slated to star in *Fiesta* (1947), a big-budget musical from MGM, but the part went to Ricardo Montalbán, who was being groomed as the latest Latin heartthrob (and who spoke much better English). It was not until *Cuban Pete,* which borrowed freely from Arnaz's nightclub act, that he was able to land a lead role. Arnaz has four songs, including two renditions of the title song, a latune classic composed by José Norman (Joseph Henderson). Although "Cuban Pete" became one of Arnaz's signature tunes, the song had been around for a while and recorded by several other artists, including Xavier Cugat, before Desi got a hold of it. More recently, it was covered by Tito Puente in *Mambo Kings* (1992) and Jim Carrey in *The Mask* (1994).

"It's Cuban! It's Cuban!" Dressed like Russian peasants, the frantic staff at Lindsay Parfums repeats the phrase as if it were a birth announcement. And in a way it is: the much-awaited new scent will be called "Cuban Rapture." Mrs. Lindsay, the owner of the company, wants Desi Arnaz (whose name "shrieks with chic") to headline the radio program where Cuban Rapture will be launched (the Cossack Choir is out). Contacted in Cuba, Desi refuses the offer because he cannot leave his orphaned niece, Brownie (another Carmelita!). Mrs. Lindsay sends Ann Williams, an account executive who looks like a fashion model, to change his mind. Although the prospect of making lots of money doesn't interest him, Ann does, and off he goes to New York with his niece and band. When Mrs. Lindsay insists on getting into his act (a harbinger of TV episodes to come), his debut is almost derailed. But after a madcap sequence that begins with Brownie's sick parrot at a gynecologist's and ends with Mrs. Lindsay in jail, the danger is averted, and Desi is a hit with New Yorkers.

Although the Latin-to-Manhattan musicals are less scenic than the weekend-in-Havana type, they come closer to speaking the truth about the underlying purpose of genre, since their plots bring Latinness home to America. Besides, it doesn't take much for tropical magic to work its effects down south, but it is indeed magic when a stateside location is turned into a Latin locale, as in the opening of *The Gang's All Here*, set on a ship that's a stage that's a "tropical spot," or as in the finale of *Too Many Girls*, which sends the students of a mythical New Mexico university into a glutinous conga frenzy. The best moment in *Cuban Pete* brings about another of these location-into-locale transformations. Rattling off the names of Latin American countries while sampling latune standards like "South American Way" and "Brazil," Arnaz takes his real and fictive audiences on a musical tour that ends in the homeland of Cuban Pete, King of the Rumba Beat. When he sings that we are now in Havana, we are; and when he adds that in Havana there's always mañana, we're happy that mañana is here and now. To my mind, the illusion of transport is all the more persuasive, the "locale color" is all the more vivid, when they arise not from newsreel clips of Latin American landmarks, however beautiful, but from the music alone. Music creates a participatory environment, a contagious feeling of otherness, that virtual sightseeing cannot accomplish. Even if the people in the nightclub or the movie theater stay put—and often they don't—they respond kinetically to the rhythm: they sway in their seats or snap their fingers or tap their feet. In John Martin's terms, they take on "a hint of the feeling that prompts the Cuban to move as he does."[6]

When Americans go south in maraca musicals, they spend a week or a weekend. Although they are tempted to stay, they always decide not to: home is where the butter is. When Latins go north, however, they not only stay but end up becoming American. This outcome reflects American ethnocentricism, of course (who wouldn't want to be a Unitedstateser?); but it also establishes a balance between America and Latin America. Each side of the cultural border receives its due: if Americans are latent Latins (a Marion Sunshine song: "The Cuban in Me"), Cubans are American wannabes. In *Cuban Pete*, Desi's band includes the El Rey Sisters, who, once they arrive in New York, are reborn as the King Sisters, a singing group that in real life performed with Arnaz's orchestra. The leader of the El Rey Sisters, Desi's old Cuban flame, dies her hair blonde and promptly acquires an Anglo boyfriend. Desi himself falls in love with Ann and never goes back to Cuba (except when he's on stage). And the denouement repeats that of *Cuban Love Song:* the orphan Brownie finds a home in the United States.

Perhaps because he was playing himself, Cuban Pete is Arnaz's most convincing role before Ricky Ricardo. Although in the 1940s he was considered a second-string Valentino, his screen persona was nothing like the Sheik's. Valentino was a sex menace. Banging on his conga drum or wiggling his hips, Desi is anything but. The romantic highpoint of *Holiday in Havana* (1949), Arnaz's last film before *I Love Lucy*, occurs when Carlos (Arnaz) and Lolita (Mary Hatcher) visit his parents. Believing that Carlos and Lolita are newlyweds, his parents escort them to the bedroom. Since Carlos doesn't dare reveal that he and Lolita aren't married, he carries her over the threshold, hesitantly. When he asks Lolita to turn the light off, she thinks he's in the mood for love—but no, he is only being a gentleman. He does sing a tender bolero, "Made for Each Other," but once the song is over he grabs a blanket, says goodnight, and goes out to sleep on the porch, which promptly collapses under him.

Like Cesar Romero before him, Arnaz is a comic caballero, a somewhat ridiculous Don Juan. It's not surprising that a Cuban singer who made his name leading conga lines in Miami Beach nightclubs did not fit the mold of the Latin Lover, whose contemporaneous avatars included Fernando Lamas, Gilbert Roland, and Ricardo Montalbán (the mysterious Mr. Roarke of TV's *Fantasy Island* clearly descended from Montalbán's Latin Lover roles). In *Cuban Pete* Desi refuses to come to the States unless he can bring Brownie. In *Holiday in Havana* we see Carlos at home with his parents and his little sister. Very much a homebody, what in Spanish is called *un muchacho de su casa*, Carlos is not likely to abduct his beloved and carry her off on a steed; he's likely to marry her. Desi always played the Latin Lover as Good

Neighbor, the Lothario next door, a role that he would perfect as Ricky Ricardo. His appeal came not from animal magnetism but from Cuban charm, which according to the authors of *Havana Mañana*, is "the country's most flourishing national industry."[7] After all, a rumba is not a tango. Smooth rather than sultry, the rumba is a dance of courtship, not possession.

Romero and Arnaz appeared together on the screen only once, in one of the last episodes of *I Love Lucy*, which by then—1957—had been retitled the *Lucy-Desi Comedy Hour*. From beginning to end, the episode has an oddly anachronistic, even elegiac tone, made all the more noticeable by the fact that the actors are much too old for the roles they play. Vacationing in Havana in 1940, Lucy and Susie (Ann Sothern) have all but given up on finding romance and rumba when they are approached by Ricky and Carlos (Arnaz and Romero), two local swells who run a sightseeing service. Although Susie and Carlos hit it off right away, Lucy and Ricky can't stand each other. Things change at a nightspot called El Tambor (what else?), where every table has the shape of a conga drum, after Ricky surprises Lucy with a bunch of violets. In one of the funniest scenes in the whole series, they then declare their love for each other with conga-drum signals. Lucy responds to Ricky's rapid-fire pounding thump for thump, until both have exhausted themselves.

A nostalgic look at the era of maraca musicals, the episode revives the conventions of the genre: the shot of the liner going past the Morro Castle, the montage of landmarks, the latune-driven dance numbers. Though now middle-aged, Desi and Cesar reprise old movie roles with energy and aplomb. As Ricky and Carlos, they sing, dance, make love—and then they emigrate to the United States when Rudy Vallee, also on vacation in Cuba, hires them to exploit the "Cuban vogue." Carlos and Ricky's opening number in the show, "Our Ship Is Coming In," literally refers to the cruise ship laden with tourists, but it also alludes to the ending, which has Carlos and Ricky fulfilling their dream of performing in the United States. Rumba-ing in El Tambor, Ricky tells Lucy that she dances well for a foreigner. "I'm not a foreigner," she replies. "I'm an American." Ricky isn't a foreigner either, he's a Cuban. Sometimes, ties of singular intimacy are nothing more complicated than two bodies swaying in 4/4 time.

Romero and Arnaz, the grandson of José Martí and the son of the mayor of the island's second largest city, Santiago de Cuba, remade the Latin Lover in Cuba's image. (To them one needs to add Estelita Rodríguez, the Cuban Fireball, whose career burned out after a few low-budget musicals and a slew of cameos in B-Westerns.) Cesar's mustache, which he refused to shave even when he played the Joker on the *Batman* TV series, made him raffish; Desi's lack of one made him boyish. Cesar never had a hair out of place; Desi's pompadour bobbed to the beat of his drum. But as natives of back-of-the-mind Cuba, both are cheerful, musical, part courtier and part clown, always safe for a turn around the dance floor or a moonlit kiss on the terrace. In an-

—Oh!. Captain. Just the last question before we land... Are Cubans very agressive?

Fig. 10. "Are Cubans Very Aggressive?" Cartoon by Conrado Massaguer. *Social*, July 1936.

other Massaguer cartoon, an American on a cruise to Havana asks the ship captain: "Oh, Captain. Just the last question before we land. Are Cubans very aggressive?" (fig. 10). Even if she is hoping for a "yes," the answer is "no." For aggressiveness, there's Argentinean Fernando Lamas, who once starred in a movie called *Jivaro* (1954), originally the name of a South American tribe but also—as *jíbaro*—slang for a wild animal or a rustic. Cuban Pete and Monte Blanca are anything but jíbaro. They may be forward, they will utter a flowery *piropo* at the drop of a straw hat, but they are not jíbaro. Like maraca musicals themselves, they are sociable, gregarious, American-friendly. Take them anywhere, New Mexico or New York, and they will set your heart a-flutter. (The butter can wait.)

FOUR
Mad for Mambo

Of all the Latin dances that, at one time or another, have migrated to the United States—the tango, the rumba, the conga, the samba, the cha-cha, the merengue—none did so more boisterously than the mambo. The rumba may have been a rage, but the mambo was madness—mambomania, the condition afflicting the thousands of Americans carried away by "that crazy out-of-this-world impossible-to-absorb mambo," in the words of Jack Kerouac.[1]

Originating in Afro-Cuban religious rituals, where the word referred to the communication between the living and the dead, by the 1930s the mambo had become attached to the final, improvised section of a *danzón*, a nineteenth-century precursor of the rumba-originating son. In the 1940s, Dámaso Pérez Prado (1916–1989), a Cuban pianist and arranger, severed the mambo from the matrix of the danzón and began to treat it as an autonomous entity. Thus the mambo was born. Unlike the son and the rumba, the mambo did not arise from a long-standing popular tradition. The first rumbas were danced on the streets; the first mambos were danced in dancehalls. The Cuban musicologist Natalio Galán likened the mambo to sugarcane juice served in plastic containers—not a bad analogy to describe the mambo's artificiality, its status as a "learned" rather than "popular" art form. Although others contributed to the concoction, it was Pérez Prado, the mambo king, who added the final ingredients, distilled it, and packaged it for consumption.

Nicknamed "Cara de foca" (Seal face), because of his small head and narrow, stooped shoulders, Pérez Prado had begun experimenting with the mixture of a big-band sound and Afro-Cuban rhythms early in his career. When Cuban record companies showed no interest in his music, considering it weird and highbrow (his favorite composer was Stravinsky), Pérez Prado moved to Mexico, where he secured a recording contract with RCA Victor. On March 30, 1949, Pérez Prado recorded the *ur*-mambo, "Qué rico el mambo," a song that took Latin America by storm. Over the next several years, he composed dozens of mambos, his press agent claiming that by 1952 Pérez Prado had sold over six million records. Even if this is hype, there is no doubt that his success was phenomenal. His popularity in Mexico was such that he required a police escort wherever he went.

Patterned after American big bands with their large reed

and brass section, Pérez Prado's orchestra departed from the Cuban model of string-heavy *charangas*. A great admirer of Stan Kenton, he used his frontline of four saxes and five trumpets in ways unheard of in Cuba. His trumpet voicings, with their dissonances and piercing high notes, and the contrapuntal scoring for brass and reeds, created a nervous intensity alien to traditional Cuban music. As freestanding fragments, Pérez Prado's mambos also lacked the two- or three-part structure of Cuban sones, and particularly the call-response chorus. A composition like "Qué rico el mambo" is a brief, brash outburst of sound, complex in its internal harmonies and dissonances but disquietingly uniform in texture. The words are minimalist to the point of absurdity. The lyric of "Qué rico el mambo" boils down to a repetition of how wonderful the mambo is: "Mambo, qué rico el mambo; mambo, qué rico es, es, es, es" (in Cuba, if a tune rocks, it's *rico*). The lyric of another famous mambo, "La niña Popoff," limits itself to repeating the girl's name over and over in the manner of scat words or trumpet stabs. The title of some of Pérez Prado's greatest mambos is only a number—"Mambo No. 5, Mambo No. 8"—a habit that reveals not only their author's artistic pretensions but his indifference toward subject matter. Laconic rather than lyrical, iterative rather than narrative, the mambo does not believe in stories. Most vocal mambos, like those which the legendary *sonero* Beny Moré recorded with Pérez Prado's orchestra, are sones or *guarachas* with mamboid flourishes. When music and words meet, the result is logoclassia, the disarticulation of language. Another famous mambo is entitled "Ni hablar" (No use talking).

Pérez Prado's new sound did not take long to reach the United States. On vacation in Mexico in 1950, bandleader Sonny Burke heard "Qué rico el mambo" and recorded it under the title "Mambo Jambo." The following year Decca released an album of Burke's mambos, most of them covers of Pérez Prado compositions that followed his arrangements closely. Encouraged by Burke's success, RCA Victor switched Pérez Prado from its international to its pop label, and his Latin American success was repeated in the United States. "Qué rico el mambo" became a hit all over again, selling upward of six hundred thousand copies, and the new rhythm became identified with the diminutive bandleader from Matanzas, Cuba, who wore zoot suits, jumped wildly onstage, and uttered strange guttural sounds that reviewers likened to "the cries of an excited muledriver" or the barks of Sharkey the Seal.[2] But in reality, Pérez Prado's trademark grunt—Ugh!—was a slurred pronunciation of the word "Dilo" (Say it!), with which he urged his musicians to give it their all (fig. 11).

With its driving Afro-Cuban percussion and aggressive brass voicings, the mambo proved irresistible. In April 1951, *Time* warned that a new dance craze was about to assault the country. Led by "Prez," as he was often called, the assault turned into a rout, with the mambo king playing to packed houses wherever he went. Reviews of the performances were glowing, with reviewers praising both the music and the showmanship. In August

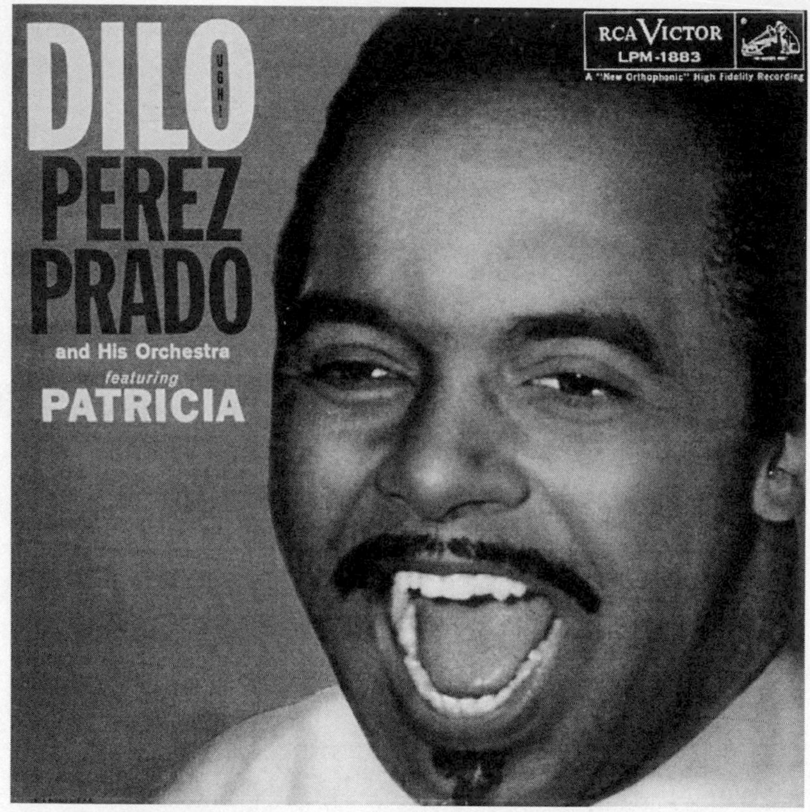

Fig. 11. Pérez Prado, album cover, *Dilo*. Courtesy Sony Music Entertainment.

1951, with Pérez Prado back for more appearances, *Variety* predicted that he was a cinch to clean up because he was as effective "on a concert date as he is on a terpery." A few months later *Down Beat* reported that Pérez Prado was proving a huge success on the West Coast, having packed thirty-five hundred gyrating dancers into Sweet's Ballroom in Oakland, the first time in many years that this had happened.[3]

By the end of 1951, mambomania had become epidemic. The largest booking agency for Latin music, Mercury Artists, added agents just for mambo orchestras and dance acts, finding them gigs in cities as diverse as Albuquerque, Las Vegas, and Indiana Harbor, Indiana. The jazz world embraced the mambo as well: Artie Shaw played "Stop and Go Mambo"; Earl Bostic recorded "Mambolino" and "Mambostic"; saxophonist Jimmy Forrest took his famed "Night Train" and turned it into "Night Train Mambo." Over the next few years almost every major American publication would run cover stories on the latest Latin dance craze, which they greeted with a mixture of fascination and puzzlement, for no one seemed quite sure what the mambo was. A 1951 *New York Times* article explained it this way: "Take the muscular contortions of the jitterbug, add the compulsive beat of African drums, find a rumba addict who has a miler's stamina and is uninhibited and double-jointed and you may soon find yourself doing the mambo." Writing in 1954, the jazz historian Nat Hentoff asserted that the mambo had become "a puzzling national enthusiasm—wildly popular but difficult to define." The mystery began with the name: some thought "mambo" was onomatopoetic, while others suggested that it was Cuban slang for "shake it."[4] Someone even ventured that it was the word uttered by Cuban peasants when cutting sugar cane ("¡mambo!" the *guajiros* would shout, as the stalks fell to the ground).

A recurring theme in the coverage was the mambo's "primitive" or "barbaric" dimension, its "lids-off demonic quality." *Ebony* began its mambo exposé: "Its impulses are frenetic, its pace is frantic, and it is called the mambo." In a pretentious essay, "The Mambo and the Mood," Barbara Squier Adler concluded: "The mambo may well be the dance-floor counterpart of psychoanalysis. Both leave, or seem to leave, the individual free of tensions acquired in trying to make a normal life in an abnormal time." So that, if ten years earlier, the rumba had allowed Americans to feel Cuban, the mambo now allowed them not to feel anything at all. Pérez Prado was dubbed "a modern pleasure god" and "a little demon," an appropriate moniker given that "diablo" had been an early synonym for mambo.[5] Since he was mulatto, racial typing undoubtedly played a part in these monikers. *Life*'s cover story for December 1954 bore the title: "Uncle Sambo, Mad for Mambo." (Already in Cuba the mambo had been considered an "africanization" of the stately danzón, which goes back to eighteenth-century English country dances.)

Ballroom dance teachers exorcized mambo devils by assuring their pupils that there were two varieties of mambo, "smooth" and "hectic." Taught at uptown dance academies like Arthur Murray's, the smooth mambo was a society dance of "subtle reasonableness." While Mrs. Arthur Murray assured potential clients that the mambo was nothing more than "rhumba—with a jitterbug accent," her husband bragged on his television show that he could teach the basic steps in under two minutes. The hectic mambo was the darker, ruder sibling. On display in venues like New York's Palladium, the Home of the Mambo, the hectic variant involved wild contortions and suggestive movements. Reading over the literature half a century later, it seems clear that no one knew exactly what the mambo was or how it should be danced. Here is one humorist's description:

> Actually the mambo is not difficult. The main part of it consists in standing in one place while a portion of the torso goes to another place. That is to say, one part of the torso starts forward and the other part, ignoring the first part, stands still. Thereupon the first part starts going backward while the second part stands still. This is followed by a rhythmic shaping of the body into the letter S and then snapping it quickly back to normal. There are more advanced steps not recommended unless accompanied by an osteopath.[6]

To be sure, the apprehension about the mambo's uninhibitedness was justified, for the mambo is indeed, as someone remarked disapprovingly, "a mockery of normal sex." Once detached from the matrix of the danzón, the mambo retained its intense, paroxysmal quality, but without the crescendo and accelerando of other genres of Cuban music. Unlike the rumba, the mambo is not a courtship dance, because courtship is segmented—a play with several acts or a symphony with several movements. The mambo knows only one act and one movement: wham-bam, thank you, mambo. The frenetic tempo of the music, the jerky bodily movements, the screeching trumpets, even Prez's famous ejaculations—all contributed to the orgiastic pitch. *Life* put it this way: "Faster and less classy than the rumba, the mambo permits its practitioners to go hog-wild with improvised solo steps while wearing an expression of ineluctable bliss."[7]

Along with repeated references to the mambo's eroticism, bizarre stories circulated in the American press about dire effects on its practitioners. It was widely reported that in Lima, in January 1951, Cardinal Juan Gualberto Guevara threatened to withhold the holy sacraments from anyone who attended Pérez Prado's performances. A few years later, the Colombian bishop Miguel Angel Builes issued an edict condemning mixed bathing, sex education, Hollywood movies, and mambo. Also in 1951 a mambo-crazed man was said to have killed several people in Mexico City. And the president of the Philippines, Ramón Magsaysay, was quoted in American newspapers as having declared the mambo a national calamity. Filipinos don't want to work, he explained, all they want to do is mambo. The strangest anecdote, however, involves a Cuban bullfighter (this is already weird enough) who claimed to have been gored by a bull because the officials at Mexico City's Plaza de Toros refused to allow the playing of a mambo while he was fighting the animal.

It did not take long for Tin Pan Alley to jump on the mambo bandwagon. As had happened with the rumba, American latunesmiths began churning out dozens of mamboids, songs that weren't mambos but alluded to them musically or in their lyrics. Most of them, like Perry Como's "Papa Loves Mambo," were amused commentaries on the mambo craze. (Someone tuning in to his TV show in 1954 would have seen Perry mamboing with Peggy Lee, whose hip action got the attention of the normally unflappable Perry.) But rather than a mambo, "Papa Loves Mambo" is an up-tempo rumba. The mambo elements in the song are citational: Afro-Cuban percussion, a few trumpet riffs, and the imitation of Pérez Prado's inimitable grunts. Of course, the mambo purists of the day fulminated against mamboids, "a wretched lot—poorly invented, poorly played, and in poor taste." No matter: in just one week in October 1954 American record companies released no fewer than ten "mambo-styled platters," and all six listings in *Downbeat's* "Everybody Dance" section for December were mambos.[8]

Besides "Papa Loves Mambo," the most successful mamboids were Vaughn Monroe's "They Were Doing the Mambo (But I Just Sat Around)," which started the genre, Rosemary Clooney's "Mambo Italiano," for a time banned from radio play because it allegedly defamed Italian Americans (sample slur: "you calabrasi do the mambo like a-crazy"), and "Show Me How to Mambo," in which an exasperated Arthur Prysock begs for an explanation of the dance. Other mamboids: "Middle Aged Mambo," "Pop 'n Mambo," "Mambo Rock," "Mambo Baby," and "Mambo Nothing." Like other latunes, some of these songs gravitated toward geography, with the difference that the locations were mostly domestic: "Manhattan Mambo," "Mississippi Mambo," "Mardi Gras Mambo," "Miami Beach Mambo." Christmas 1954 witnessed the advent of still another odd concoction, mambo Christmas carols: "Jingle Bells Mambo," "We Wanna See Santa Do the Mambo," "Rudolph the Red-Nosed Mambo," and Jimmy Boyd's "I Saw Mommy Doing the Mambo (With You Know Who)," about a boy who spies his mother getting down with Santa. Finally, as proof that the mambo was nonsectarian, the Barton Brothers came out with "Mambo Moish," and Micky Katz released "My Yiddishe Mambo," the latter about a mambonik who's "baking her *challes* for Noro Morales" (a Puerto Rican bandleader in New York). The last words of the lyric raise the hybridity of the mambo to new heights: "Olé, olé, Oy vey!"

Pérez Prado's first New York booking was at the chic Starlight Roof of the Waldorf Astoria. Initially, the mambo had been perceived as working-class, and specifically as Latin and black. When Pérez Prado opened at the Waldorf on July 27, 1954, it was a sign that the mambo had arrived. His fifteen-piece orchestra came into town primed to blow the roof off the Starlight Roof. And blow they did. Pérez Prado's may not have been the most accomplished band ever to play the Starlight, but it was certainly the loudest. Until then the Waldorf's idea of a Latin musician had been Xavier Cugat with his Mexican serapes, Chihuahuas, and tame rumbas. Even if Cugie, ever the opportunist, had already released "Mambo at the Waldorf," this was the first time that the Waldorf's well-heeled patrons got an earful of the real thing.

The reviews were favorable but wary. Praising Prez's virtuosity, reviewers remarked on Pérez Prado's startling stage antics, the variegated clothes of the "frantic horde" of mamboniks, and the "fems who shrieked in ecstasy" on hearing the vamp for "Qué rico el mambo." No question about his prowess, one critic mused, "but there's such a thing as overdoing your strength." The band was so loud, another commented, that it could be heard in Havana. During its run of several weeks, the show did good but not spectacular business. Even though *Melody Maker* maintained that Pérez Prado's booking "clinched the case for upper class patronage and a non-specialized audience," the mambo king did not play the Starlight Roof again.[9]

In July 1954, the Waldorf was only one of several mambo venues in New York. Those who found the swank Starlight Roof beyond their means did not lack for options. On Wednesday night the Palladium, which had instituted an all-mambo policy, featured Mamboscope, the weekly ballroom bacchanals where for $1.75 one could dance all night to Tito Puente's orchestra, compete in a mambo contest for amateurs, and get mambo lessons from "Killer Joe" Piro (who was Italian) and "Cuban Pete" Aguilar (who was Puerto Rican). Killer Joe, formerly a Lindy hop and jitterbug champion at the Savoy Ballroom, was the master of ceremonies. Cuban Pete and his partner, Millie Donay, blended rumba, ballroom freestyle, and acrobatics into their mambos. If the Palladium was not to your liking, you could go to Roseland, where Tito Rodríguez held court, or to the Arcadia, where Machito headlined, or to any number of smaller clubs also mad for mambo. At the Apollo in Harlem, a Cuban former welterweight champ showed off his fancy footwork in "Kid Gavilan and His Mambo Revue." Other cities had their own mambo shrines: Chicago had Mambo City, Los Angeles had Ciro's, San Francisco had the Macumba Club. In the Catskills, hotel ballrooms were full of vacationers dancing the mambo to Latin bands from New York City.

Cuba, or a certain part of Cuba, was never more evident in America than in 1954. Ernest Hemingway was awarded the Nobel Prize in Literature for *The Old Man and the Sea*, a novel about a Cuban fisherman. The top-rated program on television, *I Love Lucy*, chronicled the unpredictable home life of a Cuban bandleader and his ditsy American wife. On the radio, *Bold Venture*, a popular serial set in Havana starring Humphrey Bogart and Lauren Bacall, was in syndication. The Cuban DeCastro Sisters (no relation to bearded dictators) had a hit with "Teach Me Tonight"; the Ames Brothers with the rumba "The Naughty Lady from Shady Lane" (about a nine-day-old femme fatale); and Dean Martin with "Sway," one of the most popular latunes of all time. And in ballrooms all over the nation, the mambo craze had reached a fever pitch.

In the fall of 1954 Tico Records organized "Mambo USA," a multicity tour that began with a show at Carnegie Hall and took the mambo to America's heartland. The forty-strong mambo contingent included Machito, Joe Loco, Facundo Rivero, Miguelito Valdés, Mongo Santamaria, and the dance troupe the Mambo Aces. For Christmas, the stores were full of mambo-themed gifts: mambo dolls, mambo nighties, and mambo "kits" (a mambo record, maracas, and a plastic sheet with the dance steps on it). Paramount released *Mambo* (1954), with Silvana Mangano in the role of a dancer who has to choose between marriage and mambo. Pérez Prado himself appeared in *Underwater!* (1955)—a box-office hit for RKO whose main attraction, in addition to the music, was Jane Russell in a bathing suit. On Broadway, the musical *Damn Yankees* included a send-up of the mambo, "Who's Got the Pain (When They Do the Mambo)?" Even demure Doris Day got into the act, if somewhat belatedly, by mamboing with Gig Young in *Teacher's Pet* (1958).

By the late 1950s, however, mambomania had all but vanished, replaced by a new Cuban dance craze, the *chachachá* (or cha-cha, as it was called in English), which *Time* presciently dubbed "a beast with a future."[10] Trying to keep in step, Pérez Prado changed his tune. He retained the jazz-inspired brass but used Afro-Cuban percussion less often. By the time he recorded "Patricia" in 1958 (ironically, his biggest U.S. hit), he had added an organ and traded in his bongos and congas for trap drums and a tambourine. To hear what a difference a drum makes, it is enough to compare the original recording of "Qué rico el mambo" with the cover he did a decade later. The original arrangement is aggressive, tense, with the trumpets probing the top of their range; in the later arrangement the tempo is slower, the trumpets are mellower, and the steady thumping of the trap drums and tambourine prevents the rest of the orchestra from getting out of hand. The lyric of "Caballo negro," one of Pérez Prado's early hits, repeated one phrase: "Caballo negro que tienes la cola blanca" (Black horse with your white tail)—a metaphor that captured the Afro-Cuban-American hybridity of the classic mambos (and may also have been a reference to the slang term for cocaine, *caballo*). But in the late fifties, the white tail began to wag the black horse. In Cuba, this type of music was sometimes derided as "música de caballitos"—jingle rather than jungle music—bouncy but wearily monotonous. At its worst, the new mix sounded like the score of a bad Italian movie.

As early as 1954 the death knells for the mambo had begun pealing. Hernán Díaz, who had signed Pérez Prado for RCA Victor in 1949, was quoted in *Variety* as preferring the cha-cha because it was less vulgar. Pérez Prado responded by offering the then-considerable sum of five thousand dollars to anyone who could demonstrate that the chachachá, which was all the rage in Cuba at the time, differed significantly from his mambo.[11] To no avail: early in 1955 the trade press began to run items with such titles as "To Heck with the Mambo," "After the Mambo, What?" and "The New Hotcha: Cha Cha." The mambo king himself succumbed to the new vogue in a low-budget musical, *Cha-Cha-Boom* (1956), which some reviewers thought should have been called "Cha-Cha-Bomb." When Tommy Dorsey scored a top-ten hit with that anodyne dance-school staple, "Tea-for-Two Cha Cha," it was a sure sign that mambo madness was no more.

Even though the mambo's instrumental nature made it travel well—no need to supply an Anglophone lyric—it also limited its appeal. Unlike the rumba, which achieved its best effects by the delicate matching of words and rhythms, the mambo relied on instrumental excess. It did not lend itself to balladry, and the breathless tempo made the steps difficult to follow, much less master. The mambo was thrilling, but—as Kerouac said in *On the Road*—impossible to absorb. For this reason, in spite of its great popularity, the mambo never blended into the mainstream of American popular music; it remained essentially a novelty, an item of unassimilable exotica, as much a part of the 1950s as fall-out shelters and hula hoops.

Also derived from the *danzón*, the cha-cha was slower, more contained, its steps—one-two-cha-cha-chá—easy to learn and repeat. Equally important, the cha-cha had the good fortune to coincide with the infancy of rock and roll, to which it added Latin flavor. In his 1956 high-school yearbook, Neil Sedaka wrote that the highlight of his teenage years was "exposure to Tschaikowsky, Stravinsky and cha-cha."[12] Sure enough, several of Sedaka's early hits, beginning with "Oh, Carol" and "Stairway to Heaven," were cha-chas. A few years later, rock-and-roller Sam Cooke observed that "Everybody Loves to Cha Cha Cha"—a title become reality in doo-wop standards like "Stay" and "Little Darlin'" and pop ballads like "Diana" and "Johnny Angel."

"Mashed Potato Time," Dee Dee Sharp's 1962 hit, discloses that "the Mashed Potato started a long time ago / with a guy named Sloppy Joe." The reference to the famous Havana bar is a veiled acknowledgment that, musically, mashed-potato time descends from cha-cha time, as does "The Loco-Motion," another popular 1962 record whose punning title winks at the song's origins. That same year Bobby Rydell had a top-ten hit whose heritage was not veiled at all—"The Cha-Cha-Cha," which proclaims the superiority of the cha-cha over the twist. (Connie Francis decided to have it both ways with the "Cha Cha Twist.") And let's not forget the baby-cha quintuplets: "There Goes My Baby" (The Drifters), "Take Good Care of My Baby" (Bobby Vee), "Be My Baby" (The Ronettes), "Don't Worry Baby" (The Beach Boys), and "Baby I'm Yours" (Barbara Lewis). Or the cha-cha-charged rockabilly of Roy Orbison in songs like "Blue Bayou," "Only the Lonely," "In Dreams," and "Falling." Or every hit The Four Seasons ever had. By the mid-1960s, the beast with a future had become so domesticated that its lurking in The Beatles' "And I Love Her" and Frank Sinatra's "Strangers in the Night" went unnoticed. As it did, a couple of years later, in Van Morrison's "Brown Eyed Girl," The Rascals' "Groovin'," and The Captain and Tenille's "Love Will Keep Us Together" (composed, not coincidentally, by Neil Sedaka).

Although its progeny is not as plentiful, the mambo also did not vanish from America's imagination, or from its songbook. In the movie *Dirty Dancing* (1987), Patrick Swayze played a Catskills dance instructor who teaches Jennifer Grey how to do "Johnny's Mambo." A year earlier, the theme song of Jonathan Demme's *Something Wild* (1986) had been the mambo "Loco de amor," composed by David Byrne and Johnny Pacheco and sung by Byrne along with Celia Cruz. One of the cuts in Barry Manilow's *Swing Street* (1987), "Hey Mambo," used Cuban percussion and mambo vamps to tell the story of "the king of Latin swing." After Oscar Hijuelos won the Pulitzer Prize for *The Mambo Kings Play Songs of Love* (1989), a novel about two Cuban brothers who ride the mambo wave of the 1940s and 1950s, the movie version of the novel recreated the Palladium, where a horde of mamboniks danced again to the timbales of Tito Puente, who played himself. Inspired by the popularity of Hijuelos's novel, New Yorkers began once more taking mambo lessons and displaying their moves in Manhattan nightclubs—a revival that made its way into *The Simpsons*, with Homer listing the mambo among his favorite pastimes, along with bowling and munching Pork Rinds Lite. And then, in 1999, fifty years after Pérez Prado recorded "Qué rico el mambo," the mambo came alive again in Lou Bega's best-selling cover of "Mambo No. 5," which supplemented Prez's original with hip-hop lyrics. The madness may have been temporary, but the beat goes on.

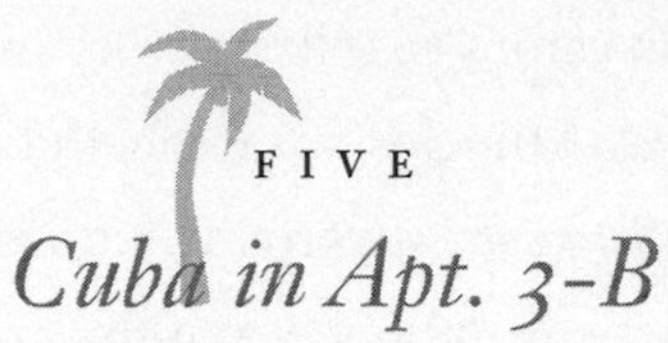

FIVE

Cuba in Apt. 3-B

Lucy to Ricky: Don't jabber at me in a foreign tongue.
Ricky to Lucy: It's not a foreign tongue, it's Spanish.

A few months before his death in 1986, Desi Arnaz remarked that he wanted to be remembered as the "I" in *I Love Lucy*—a wish that was both self-affirming and self-effacing, for it is not so easy to determine who is the "I" in *I Love Lucy.* Since the show exploited the resemblances between the fictional lives of the characters (Lucy and Ricky Ricardo) and the real life of the actors (Lucille Ball and Desi Arnaz), the "I" refers to Ricky as well as to Desi. In addition, from the beginning of the show's phenomenal run, the "I" was appropriated by the millions of Lucy fans. Jack Gould, the TV critic for the *New York Times*, put it this way: "*I Love Lucy* is probably the most misleading title imaginable. For once, all available statistics are in agreement: Millions love Lucy."[1] In the 1950s, the Chicago department store Marshall Field's decided to close early on Monday nights because most of its customers were staying home to watch the program. The sign in the store said, "We love Lucy too, so we're closing on Monday nights." Lucy's fan club was, of course, the We Love Lucy Fan Club. And the series was broadcast on CBS, whose famous corporate logo, a gigantic eye, was first used in September 1951, only a month before the show went on the air.

All of which makes Desi something of an invisible man, the owner of an "I" that nobody sees, since the title refers as much to him and Ricky as to the "eye" of the show's beholders, whose iconographic rendering was the CBS eye.

The story behind the title is well known: CBS wanted Lucille Ball to do a television version of her radio show, *My Favorite Husband*, in which Richard Denning played her husband. Ball agreed, but only if Desi Arnaz took Denning's part. Since the radio program was about an American housewife and her husband, the network balked, fearing that Arnaz would not be credible as the husband. In *My Favorite Husband*, Denning was a waspish banker from Minneapolis—hardly a suitable role for a conga player from Cuba. After the program's concept was modified to fit Arnaz's background, the network finally agreed, but without much enthusiasm. Ball and Arnaz would play a show-biz couple; the husband would be a struggling bandleader whose zany wife would try anything to get into his act—a plot idea borrowed, perhaps, from *Cuban Pete*, where Mrs. Lindsay, of Lindsay Parfum fame, tried every which way to get into Desi's act.

What to call the show remained a problem, however. Mindful

of Desi's ego, Ball's first impulse was to call it *The Desi Arnaz–Lucille Ball Show*, a feckless title to which the network objected, since she was the drawing card for the series. At the time Arnaz was known, if at all, as the leader of a Latin orchestra and a minor movie actor. By contrast, Lucille Ball was the "Queen of the B-pictures," a bankable actress, if not quite a star, whose Hollywood career gave the new medium the legitimacy it was seeking. After much discussion, Jess Oppenheimer, the producer, came up with the clever compromise: "I Love Lucy." Leaving the spotlight on his more famous wife, the sentence gave Desi pride of place but without actually naming him. It does take a moment's reflection to realize who is the "I" in *I Love Lucy*.

And yet Arnaz's TV persona, Ricky Ricardo, has been the single most influential Hispanic in the history of the United States. By now several generations of Americans have acquired many of their notions of how Cuban men behave, how they talk, lose their temper, treat or mistreat their wives, by watching Ricky love Lucy. Not even Fidel Castro, that charismatic *comandante*, has exercised an equal hold on the American imagination. For millions of Americans—and not a few Cuban Americans—Ricky Ricardo has become the quintessential Cuban, charming but volatile, familiar but foreign. Some years ago I had a student at Duke University who confessed that he had learned to be Cuban by watching *I Love Lucy* reruns from his home in Hialeah.

I Love Lucy went on the air on October 15, 1951. It ran for six seasons, during which 180 half-hour episodes were broadcast.

Between 1957 and 1960 the show was rebaptized *The Lucy-Desi Comedy Hour*, and thirteen hour-long episodes aired at irregular intervals. The last episode was filmed on March 2, 1960, coincidentally the day of Desi Arnaz's forty-third birthday and, not coincidentally, the day before Lucille Ball filed for divorce after a tumultuous twenty-year marriage. During four of its six seasons (including the last), *I Love Lucy* was the highest rated show on television and never dropped lower than third. There were Monday nights when eight out of ten TVs in America were tuned in to the antics of Lucy and Ricky. Between 9:00 and 9:30, telephone calls across the nation plummeted, as did the water flush rate. In January 1953, the episode in which Lucy gave birth to little Ricky drew forty-four million viewers, many more than saw the Eisenhower inauguration a day earlier. Legend has it that even Mamie Eisenhower took time off from the inaugural celebrations to watch the blessed event. Americans may have liked Ike, but they loved Lucy.

At last count the show has been broadcast in seventy-seven countries and translated into twenty-one languages, including Spanish. Since its premiere, it has never been off the air in Southern California; in 1980 someone calculated that episodes from *I Love Lucy* had been shown in Washington, D.C., a total of 3,704 times—which may help explain U.S. policy toward Cuba. The show's stars have been the subject of made-for-TV movies, documentaries, and many books. In Oscar Hijuelos's *Mambo Kings Play Songs of Love*, the high point in the careers of Cesar and

Nestor Castillo, the fictional mambo kings, is a cameo appearance on *I Love Lucy* as Ricky's Cuban cousins. The Cuban-born rapper Mellow Man Ace calls himself "The Ricky Ricardo of Rap," wrote a song entitled "Babalú Bad Boy," and named his son Desi (as did actress Jaime Pressly). Eddie Murphy's *Delirious* includes an over-the-top impersonation of Ricky—"a cool motherfucker"—singing "Cuban Cabby." Lucy and Desi grace postage stamps and lottery tickets. In 2001, to commemorate the fiftieth anniversary of the show, a replica of the *I Love Lucy* set toured the country, allowing fans to reenact favorite scenes. All sorts of *I Love Lucy* paraphernalia are available on the Web: dolls, placemats, pillows, pajamas, playing cards, Halloween costumes—not to mention the Vitameatavegamin tonic made famous in one of the show's episodes. The series has even spawned porn videos with titles like *Lucy Has a Ball* and *Lucy Makes It Big.*

On the face of it, *I Love Lucy* is an unlikely candidate for such success. Its strength has been considered the light-hearted portrayal of the trials and tribulations of a typical American couple. In the 1950s, the *New York Times* quoted a British anthropologist: "Lucy and Ricky and their friends Ethel and Fred are the typical American middle class, in a typical middle-class environment. But with this significant difference. Instead of sitting around waiting for things to happen, they make things happen. They and their audience are so alike, the audience comes to believe that it is *it* that makes thing happen." But Lucy and Ricky are unlikely choices as comic doubles for the folks next door. After all, the show went on the air during the Eisenhower era, a conformist age that embraced American values and persecuted un-American activities. Nonetheless, the TV hit of the decade, a show that the Museum of Broadcasting has labeled "The Mona Lisa of television," featured a couple whose husband made a living singing "Babalú"—not exactly an American activity.[2] Incongruously, the typical couple of the Eisenhower era consisted of a redhead from New York and a conga-thumping Lothario from Cuba with a slick pompadour and a precarious command of the English language. (A sign on Desi's dressing room door warned: English is broken here.)

The typical *I Love Lucy* episode centers on some form of competition between Ricky and Lucy. Desi thinks housework is easy, Lucy disagrees. Lucy wants to go to the movies, Desi wants to go to the fights. Desi will let Lucy appear in his act, but she has to fit into a size 12. The battle lines are well drawn: on one side, Lucy and Ethel; on the other, Ricky and Fred. Usually the trouble arises from the supposedly irreducible differences between husbands and wives, or men and women. In some episodes, however, the conflict emerges from the clash of cultures. Ricky is not just male but Cuban. Lucy is not just female but American. What puts them at loggerheads is not only gender but nationality. In these episodes the overriding theme is not the war of the sexes but what Lucy called the "battle of the accents."

This phrase occurs in "Lucy Hires an English Tutor," an episode from the second season about her efforts to improve Ricky's

English. As the episode begins, a very pregnant Lucy sits in the living room knitting something for the baby. Ricky comes in with a "papaya-juice milk shake," into which she dips a dill pickle.[3] The conversation turns to the sex of their child. Every man wants a boy, she says, so that he can see himself running around; every woman wants a girl, he retorts, so that she can teach her how to catch a man. Ricky volunteers that his son will attend his alma mater, "Havana U," and launches into a rendition of his school anthem—"Havana U, la mejor eres tú"—which he sings to the tune of the Michigan fight song. This gets them into an argument about how Ricky's deficient English will affect their child's upbringing. After Ricky tries unsuccessfully to pronounce such words as "bough," "rough," "through," and "cough" (which he pronounces "buff," "row," "thruff," and "coo"), he concludes that since English is a "crazy language," his son will speak Spanish instead. Lucy will have none of it—this is America, where people speak English—and pledges to hire an English tutor so that anyone who converses with her son will speak perfect English.

In the next scene we are back in the living room with the English tutor, Mr. Livermore (Hans Conried), a stuffy pedant with a fastidious pronunciation and a hysterical aversion to slang. After a few funny scenes where Mr. Livermore attempts to correct Ricky's diction and accent, the lessons come to an unexpected conclusion: instead of improving Ricky's English, Mr. Livermore ends up sounding like Ricky. When he launches into an ear-splitting rendition of "Babalú," Lucy calls the whole thing off. "Ok, ok," she says, "It was a battle of the accents and Mr. Livermore lost."

In a show that has been criticized for its ethnocentrism, Lucy's admission of defeat marks an interesting moment. Rather than persisting in her efforts to "Americanize" her husband, she gives in. The reason is that, as many episodes make clear, Lucy loves Ricky because he is *not* American. In 1950, as part of their campaign to do a TV show together, Lucy and Desi put together a vaudeville sketch in which they played Cuban Pete, the King of the Rumba Beat, and Sally Sweet, the Queen of Delancey Street. Straw hat in hand, Cuban Pete begins to sing his song, but then Sally enters, and the rumba segues into a swing. At first, Pete and Sweet can't get their act together. He steps on his lines and she steps on his toes. But little by little, Sally starts to sway, and by the end of the number the two of them are chick-chicky-booming in unison. Cuban Pete and Sally Sweet foretell Ricky and Lucy.

"Ricky Minds the Baby" (January 18, 1954) culminates in a brilliant long scene during which Ricky narrates the story of *Little Red Riding Hood*—in Spanish. His *Caperucita roja* contains enough English to be intelligible—"Granmamá, pero what big ojos tú tienes!"—but otherwise the viewer is subjected to almost five minutes of Spanish. It's an unusual scene not only because of its language but because of its location. Although the apartment is normally Lucy's domain, in this scene it is Ricky who occupies the spotlight, while Lucy—for once a willing bystander—listens behind the door with Fred and Ethel. In addition, Ricky's performance borrows Lucy's best resource, impersonation, for as he tells the story he jumps around the room like the wolf or cowers like Little Red Riding Hood. Ricky's Spanish-language utterances are usually song lyrics or rapid-fire tirades. Combining the familiarity of the song lyric with the spontaneity of the tirade, his bedtime story demonstrates that his native tongue can be used for purposes other than romance or remonstrance. And the Spanish storytelling must have had an effect, for in a later episode Lucy mentions that little Ricky cries with a Cuban accent.

But what if Livermore's lessons had succeeded? What if Lucy had won the battle of the accents? Given the importance of Ricky's voice in the show, such an outcome is unimaginable. Since Lucille Ball excelled at slapstick comedy—disguises, pratfalls, stunts—it is easy to overlook the significance of Ricky's aural presence. Lucy clowns, Ricky croons. Lucy is a genius with props; Ricky has a gift for malapropisms. While Lucy mugs, Ricky goes "¡ay, ay, ay, ay!" and breaks out in Spanish. We remember Lucy for her wonderful repertoire of "faces," to which the show's writers assigned names: "Puddling Up" (on the verge of tears), "Spider" (just got caught), "Umlaut" (crosses her eyes), "Drats" (makes a fist in frustration), "Double drats" (two fists). But what we remember about Ricky is the sound of his voice. His signature is aural, not visual. He walks into the apartment, drops his coat on the sofa, and says those immortal words: “Lucy, I’m home.”

Like other appearances of back-of-the-mind Cuba, *I Love Lucy*’s is generally stereotypical and often condescending. Ricky’s accent—the *Los Angeles Times* called it “the Arnaz-ization of the American language”—and his vaunted malapropisms—“Birds of a feather smell the same,” “I’ll cross that bridge when I burn it”—provided an inexhaustible source of cheap laughs.[4] All Lucy had to do was mimic Ricky’s “dunts” and “wunts” and the audience’s amused response was automatic. Nevertheless, episodes like “Lucy Hires an English Tutor” and “Ricky Minds the Baby” not only raise the issue of what today we would call multiculturalism but resolve it in Ricky’s favor.

Enlivening every argument and every reconciliation, Ricky’s Cubanness is a crucial component in the “I” of *I Love Lucy*. Beginning with the mambo-inflected theme song, Cuba is everywhere. When Ricky makes a toast, it’s “a Cubita bella.” When Christmas arrives, he sings a “wonderful Cuban melody,” “Cascabel” (“Jingle Bells”), that the Americans have stolen. When he finds Lucy with her supposed French paramour, he threatens to hit him over the head with his conga drum. “We’re going to run this home like we do in Cuba,” Ricky says, “where the man is the master and the woman does what she is told” (“Equal Rights,” October 23, 1953).

For her part, Lucy never tires of bringing up Ricky’s nationality. Hungry, he is "a starving Cuban." Befuddled, he's a "poor confused Cuban." Sly, he's a "conniving Cuban." Angry, he's in a "Cuban snit." With tousled hair, he is "a funny-looking Cuban." In a tux, he's a "Cuban dreamboat." When she thinks he's two-timing her, he degenerates into "Cuban heel." But once she discovers her mistake, she cooks him his favorite dish, *arroz con pollo* (yellow rice and chicken). Anytime they make coffee for guests, it's espresso, served in the tiny cups and saucers used by Cubans. An aspiring playwright, Lucy pens an opus entitled "A Tree Grows in Havana."

And then there is Ricky's home away from home, the Tropicana, named after its Havana namesake (and later renamed Club Babalu), the site of the most touching moment in the entire series, Lucy's announcement that she's going to have a baby. At the Tropicana we find the only other Cuban with a recurring role, Marco Rizo, Desi Arnaz's longtime pianist, who occasionally has a line or two. When Ricky speaks Spanish at home, he is talking to himself. Even telling the story of *Caperucita roja*, he is talking to himself. But Spanish is the Tropicana's native language. If Apt. 3-B is Ricky's America in microcosm, the Tropicana is his portable Cuba. When Ricky gets fed up with show business, he buys a diner and greets his clients in a tuxedo just as he did at the club. The diner's name: "A Little Bit of Cuba."

Along with the kitchen, the living room, and the bedroom of the apartment, the Tropicana was one of the four basic sets in the show. Placed side by side on the Desilu soundstage, their contiguity signaled the intimacy of apartment and nightclub. As the Cuban room in the Ricardo household, the nightclub extended its influence—its atmosphere—to the rest of the residence. 3-B may be Lucy's turf, but Cuba permeates the household: from the painting of a colonial town on the wall (Santiago de Cuba, Desi's birthplace?) to the conga drum behind the front door. Ricky's band performs several times in the apartment, once playing a "farewell dirge" to Lucy, who believes she is dying of a rare tropical disease. Ricky may not always run his home the way he would have in Cuba, but he is its tutelar spirit, the Mr. Cuba of Apt. 3-B.

During the six seasons of *I Love Lucy*, the Ricardos traveled far and wide. In the fourth season they took a cross-country trip to Los Angeles so that Ricky could star in a movie about Don Juan (that never came off). The following season they toured Europe, stopping in England, Paris, the Swiss Alps, and Italy, where Lucy learned to stomp grapes. In light of this wanderlust, it is odd that the Ricardos went to Cuba only one time, in an episode from the final season. The visit occurs during the Ricardos' Florida vacation, which they interrupt so that, after fifteen years of marriage, Lucy can finally meet her husband's family ("The Ricardos Visit Cuba," December 3, 1956). For once, Lucy is the foreigner and Ricky is on home turf. Now the jokes are about *her* accent, not his. As one would expect, the visit doesn't go well, for Lucy runs afoul of Ricky's relatives, and particularly Uncle Alberto, the patriarch of the family, whose expensive Cuban cigars she inadvertently crushes. When she tries to replace them, she makes the situation worse by impersonating a cigar roller and wreaking havoc in a cigar store.

But then again, family is a difficult subject on *I Love Lucy*. Although there are many references to Ricky's relatives, Ricky's mother visits them only once, with dire consequences, and Lucy's mother, Mrs. McGillicuddy, puts in a few appearances that do not go any better. For the most part Lucy and Ricky are accompanied only by Fred and Ethel, who seem even more bereft of family than the Ricardos.

On the plane down to Cuba, Ricky reads little Ricky a booklet called "The Three of Us." Nervous about the visit, Lucy asks about Ricky's Cuban family, whereupon he starts reciting the names of aunts, uncles, nieces, nephews, and cousins. The scene poignantly contrasts the nuclear family of the storybook's title—represented by Lucy, Ricky, and little Ricky—with the extended family more typical of Cubans and other Latin Americans. In the course of the episode, these two concepts of family play off against each other, as Ricky goes back and forth between his Cuban and his American family. In some scenes, he is Lucy's husband; in others, he is his father's son. His bilingual name signifies this dual identity: Ricardo is the Cuban man; Ricky is the American husband. Ricky Ricardo is the Cuban-American man and husband.

Like many others, this episode concludes with a song, except that Ricky is not at the Tropicana but in the nightclub of Havana's Hotel Nacional. He sings a latune composed especially for the occasion, "Un hombre afortunado" ("A Lucky Guy"), which lists the advantages of a bicultural life like his:

I have two places to hang my hat,
two verandas in which to snooze,
and in two languages a welcome mat:
say hello to my shoes.

After he finishes the song, little Ricky comes on stage with a child-sized conga drum (the same one on which his father learned to play), and the two of them pound out a few choruses of "Babalú"—proof, Ricky says, that although his son was born in the United States, "there is a lot of Cuba in his heart." Once the father-son duet concludes, Lucy joins them on stage, and it's "the three of us" together again as Uncle Alberto and the rest of Ricky's Cuban relatives watch from the audience. One could imagine a different finale, in which the whole extended family goes up to take a bow, but that would go against the grain of the show. Although *I Love Lucy* nods toward Ricky's extended family, it affirms the primacy of the nuclear unit.

Although in "Un hombre afortunado" Ricky claims that he has two homes, in fact he has only one. Cuba is a frame of reference, a source of identity, a term of comparison, but it's not a home. The reason the Ricardos visit Cuba in only one of the 180 episodes is that Desi's character—like Desi himself—had no interest in regression (in Spanish, *regreso* is return). Ricky is in America to stay. When he arrives in Cuba, he doesn't say, as he might have, "Lucy, I'm home."

In the second episode of the series, "Be a Pal" (October 22, 1951), Lucy is worried that Ricky has become bored with her. She tries different tricks to rekindle his interest. First she greets him in the morning wearing a tight-fitting sequined gown, but he doesn't look up from his newspaper. Next she tries playing poker with Ricky and his pals, but that turns out badly when she beats the boys. Finally, at Ethel's urging, she decides that the way to get his attention is to mother him, to "treat him like a baby and surround him with things that remind him of his childhood." In the next scene the wonderfully adaptable living room has become a Cuban theme park, or Lucy's idea of one: a chicken coop, bananas, a couple of palm trees, and a crouching mannequin with serape and sombrero. Knowing that Ricky's mother was a famous singer and dancer, Lucy dresses up as Carmen Miranda. When Ricky walks in after a hard day of rehearsals, Lucy sambas out of the bedroom singing the Brazilian standard "Mamâe eu quero," a song that Miranda made famous in *Down Argentine Way.* As Lucy goes into her dance, five boys—Pedro, Pablo, Chucho, Jacinto, y José—run out into the living room and converge on Ricky (the names of Ricky's brothers were not picked at random; they come from "Mis cinco hijos" [My five sons], a guaracha by the Cuban composer Osvaldo Farrés). Bug-eyed, Ricky asks Lucy whether she has gone off her rocker. Lucy explains: "I thought you were getting tired of me and if I reminded you of Cuba you might like me better." Ricky's response: "Lucy, honey, if I wanted things Cuban I'd have stayed in Havana. That's the reason I married you, 'cause you're so different from everyone I'd known in Cuba." (To which Lucy answers: "Who'd you know in Cuba?")

If Lucy loves Ricky because he's Cuban, Ricky loves Lucy because she is not. One doesn't have to watch many episodes of the show to notice Ricky's fascination with Americana and, more pointedly, with *americanas*—those "glorious 'honks' of stuff" that he drools over. "Whenever he sees a pretty girl," Lucy says, "he becomes more Cuban." And the prettier the girl, the thicker his accent. In one respect, *I Love Lucy* is a theater of domestic war; in another, it is the great Cuban-American love story, a chronicle of how a Cuban man and an American woman made a life together.

Remember how each episode ends: Lucy and Ricky make up, clinch, and kiss. After the kiss, the next thing we see is a heart superimposed on rumpled satin sheets and then the show's title, *I Love Lucy*. Stripped to its literal core, the title of the series is quite racy, for it is in the bedroom that Ricky *really* loves Lucy. In his memoirs, Desi states: "I think the audience could visualize Lucy and Ricky going to bed together and enjoying it."[5] Fred could visualize it too; he calls Lucy and Ricky "lovebirds" who are "at it" all the time. *I Love Lucy* is not just a show about domestic trials and tribulations but, as in the title, about love. There is a world of difference between *My Favorite Husband*, the title of Lucille Ball's radio program, and that of the TV series, for *I Love Lucy* defines Ricky not as husband, not as father, not as entertainer, but only as lover. His "I" is a lover's I. Even though Lucy and Ricky slept in twin beds, who can doubt that they spent their nights making crossover dreams come true?

These erotic undertones make *I Love Lucy* an unusual exemplar of the fifties sitcom. Putting the focus on domestic travails or family affection, the other family-themed shows of that era convey a different message. Think, for example of the celebrated opening of Jackie Gleason's *The Honeymooners:* a splash of fireworks, followed by a skyline with a moon rising behind it. Tondo-like, the moon serves as a frame for Jackie Gleason's face, then for his name and the title of the show, and finally for the names of the other actors. Although the initial image of exploding fireworks goes along with the title's romantic connotations, the skyline establishes a social rather than a marital setting. As viewers, we find ourselves not in the privacy of an apartment, and certainly not in the intimacy of a bedroom, but in the midst of skyscrapers and highrises. And by using the rising moon as a frame for Gleason's mug, the show shifts our attention from a couple of honeymooners to one star. After a few seconds into the opening credits, the pilot metaphor has changed from that of the "honeymoon" to that of the "man on the moon." Since the Kramdens are a far cry from honeymooning lovebirds, the comic reversal of the opening images prepares us for the diverting but dreary lives of Ralph and Alice.

Or consider another hit sitcom from that era, *Make Room for Daddy*, a show inspired by the success of *I Love Lucy* and filmed at the Desilu studios. Like the Ricardos, the Williamses are a show-biz family living in an apartment in New York. Just as Ricky Ricardo is Desi Arnaz's TV twin, Danny Williams is Danny Thomas's. If Ricky headlines at the Tropicana, Danny does the same at the Club Copa. And since Danny is Lebanese, his ethnic idiosyncrasies are a recurring motif and a running gag. But the one fundamental difference is that, from the title onward, *Make Room for Daddy* highlights Danny's role as a devoted family man. Danny and Daddy are the same person, and almost the same word. The show's opening underscores this: as Danny walks in through the door, his wife comes out of one room and his two children from another. They meet in the center of the living room and fall back together onto the sofa—quite a contrast with the rumpled satin sheets of *I Love Lucy*. *Make Room for Daddy* begins and ends with the family gathering in the living room; *I Love Lucy*, with Lucy and Ricky together in bed.

What sets *I Love Lucy* apart, in addition to the talent of its stars, is the aura and allure of "things Cuban." Lucy and Ricky are not, as the reviewers liked to say, a typical middle-class American couple—not because they are not middle-class, but because they are not American; they are Cuban American. In the Ricardo household, the battle of the accents spices the war of the sexes. When Mr. Livermore asks Ricky where he acquired his "odd pronunciation," Ricky replies: "I was born in Cuba, what your 'scuse?" The answer not only puts Livermore in his place but provides the excuse or, rather, the explanation for the uniqueness of the show. Those executives skeptical that Americans would accept a Cuban as Lucille Ball's TV husband did not reckon with the singular intimacy of the ties between the two countries. Ricky and Lucy's marriage offers yet another example, perhaps the most compelling, of the erotics of Cuban-American relations, an economy of desire that goes back to the exuberant accounts of nineteenth-century travelers like William Henry Hurlbert, for whom Cuba was a fair Odalisque, and recurred throughout the first half of the twentieth century in countless movies, songs, tourist guides, and magazine and newspaper articles. A lucky, lusty couple, Lucy and Ricky acted out their version of this centuries-long romance on those rumpled satin sheets that have become an enduring American icon.

SIX

Dirges in Bolero Time

"You know how it is there early in the morning in Havana"—so begins Ernest Hemingway's *To Have and Have Not* (1937), relying on that back-of-the-mind familiarity that Americans had with Cuba. Except that Hemingway's Havana is not the city where, as the sun rises behind the Morro, the cries of peanut vendors fill the air and American tourists tumble from cruise ships. On that morning in Havana, three young men will be shot dead as they walk out of a café, gunned down by a rival political faction, or perhaps by the government's own henchmen.

Rather than the safe haven of latunes and maraca musicals, the Havana of *To Have and Have Not* is a venue for murder and corruption; the principals are gun-runners and revolutionaries, gamblers and gold diggers, pimps and B-girls. This is the Havana of crime and mystery novels: George Harmon Coxe's *Murder in*

Havana (1943) and *Woman at Bay* (1945), Cornell Woolrich's *Black Path of Fear* (1944), Charles Booth's *Mr. Angel Comes Aboard* (1944), Robert Sylvester's *Rough Sketch* (1948) and *The Big Boodle* (1954), Richard Powell's *Shot in the Dark* (1952), and Frances and Richard Lockridge's *Voyage into Violence* (1956). It is also the Havana of a handful of mostly forgettable movies: *Her Man* (1930), *The Shady Lady* (1930), *The Chase* (1946), *We Were Strangers* (1949), *The Bribe* (1949), *A Lady without Passport* (1950), *Sarumba* (1950), and *The Gun Runners* (1958). In their big-screen incarnations, both the "Thin Man" and the "Lone Wolf" solved murders involving Cuban gangsters, as did Bob Hope—comically—in *The Ghost Breakers* (1940). In *Key Largo* (1948), mobster Johnny Rocco has just returned from Havana with a hundred thousand dollars' worth of funny money. In *The Miami Story* (1954), the gangsters are Cuban, but they meet Rocco's fate just the same when they are killed at the Miami airport.

No less a fantasy setting, a locale, than the pleasure capital of the tourist guides, noir Havana—Wallace Stevens might have called it "lunar Havana"—plays off Cuba's reputation as "a magic land, all green and gay, the wonderland to which every dream led."[1] This sentence is spoken by Julie Avery, one of the protagonists of Elinor Rice's *Action in Havana*, a single thirty-something who finally has the chance to visit the land of her dreams. The man to whom she is speaking, an American journalist, tells her that if she pries beneath the surface, she will find that Cuba the Beautiful—Ricky Ricardo's *Cubita bella*—is an illusion. This clash between expectation and reality (fictional reality) generates noir Havana stories. The tourist attractions remain the same, but they acquire a different cast. At Sloppy Joe's, people get murdered. In the Morro Castle, political dissidents languish. At once fun house and horror show, America's smartest city has become sinister, duplicitous. The sunny isle has turned lunatic. Although femme fatales abound, as they always do in the noir genre, the ultimate femme fatale is La Habana herself, irresistible but lethal.

In Cornell Woolrich's best-selling *Black Path of Fear*, which inspired the movie *The Chase* (1946) as well as a radio play starring Cary Grant, the protagonist's girlfriend is stabbed at Sloppy Joe's while "Siboney," the dreamy tune that Bing Crosby crooned, plays in the background. The same song that transported latune lovers to dreamland now provides the musical accompaniment to murder. And appropriately so, for Lecuona's tune "makes a good dirge. It breaks your heart for you." According to Dashiell Hammett, in the 1940s a certain funeral parlor in Havana had a bar inside it. True or not, the anecdote provides an apt metaphor for noir Havana, hedonistic but dangerous, where at any moment you can step "out of the brightness of holiday into the darkness of murder."[2]

In Woolrich's novel, Scotty and Lorna go to Cuba after she has left her sadistic husband. As they are about to toast her freedom, she falls to the floor. Scotty looks down at a pool of blood. It takes him a moment to realize what has happened: an invisible hand plunged a knife into Lorna—the same knife, apparently, that he had just bought in a Chinese curio store. In the end Scotty is cleared of the murder by a photograph that shows something no one at the crowded bar was able to see: a stranger's arm digging into Lorna's side. It is always like this in noir Havana; reality needs to be made visible, as if all of the city were an immense darkroom. In Spanish, to develop a photograph is *revelar*, to reveal. A place famous for sightseeing is now full of sights unseen, negatives in need of revelation.

As he traverses the lantern-lit alleys of Havana's Chinatown, Scotty finds it difficult to navigate the crush of bodies redolent of sweat and alcohol. The air is almost unbreathable. The narrow streets are almost impassable. No ñango-induced reveling here. No romantic antics by the likes of Cesar Romero and Carmen Miranda. Tropical magic has turned black. (Appropriately, the mysterious woman who helps Scotty beat the rap is a prostitute nicknamed Medianoche, "Midnight.") Instead of an enticing exoticism, Havana offers a menacing foreignness; that is, a foreignness completely unlike that of Massaguer's rumbera poster. On the night that Lorna, a tourist trapped, is murdered, the movie theater nearby is showing *Volando a Río* (*Flying Down to Rio*)—one more way in which Woolrich makes the point that his story is not escapist fare, at least not of the Fred and Ginger variety. Engaged in a different kind of flight, Scotty and Lorna find that Havana offers no escape. The lesson seems to be: don't trust the dreamland, for at any time it can become a nightmare scenario. Like other paradises (in the noir context, Raymond Chandler's California comes to mind), Havana has a deadly underside.

The most accomplished movie about lunar Havana, John Huston's *We Were Strangers* (1949), involves the building of a tunnel to facilitate the assassination of dictator Gerardo Machado, who ruled Cuba between 1925 and 1933. Most of the action transpires underground, in a subterranean labyrinth that literally underlies the bright tropical paradise. It's not only the two protagonists of the movie, Tony Fenner (John Garfield) and China Valdés (Jennifer Jones), who are strangers: underground Havana—which is also the Havana of the anti-Machado underground—has become estranged from its tourism-engendered twin. In 1930 the *Washington Post* reported that half of the Cubans spent their time entertaining tourists and the other half making revolution. Of course this is a caricature; most Cubans, then as now, spend their time doing other things. But the statement reinforces the idea of two disparate cities occupying the same location. In *Havana Mañana*, May and Hermer make the same point with a light-heartedness that borders on the offensive: of the Cuban three "r's," the first two are Rum and Rumba; the third is Revolution.[3] (May and Hermer could not have anticipated, of course, that the most recent Cuban revolution, unlike its short-lived predecessors, would span more than half a century.)

Loosely based on Sylvester's *Rough Sketch*, *We Were Strangers* was one of the few flops that John Huston made in the 1940s (his previous movie had been *Key Largo;* his next would be *The As-*

phalt Jungle). It seems that nobody wanted to see Havana from the bottom up. Not only did moviegoers stay away, but reviewers panned the picture for spreading communist propaganda—"the heaviest dish of Red theory ever served to an audience outside the Soviet."[4] The charge arose from the movie's advocacy of violent resistance to tyranny. One character's reasoning: "If you're willing to give an innocent life for your country, your own, why aren't you willing to take one?" In the Hemingwayesque ending, as Tony lies dying after a shoot-out with the police, morning breaks over the city. People pour into the streets. Church bells begin to peal. Conga lines form to the chant of "¡Viva la revolución!"—for the dictator has fled. Seeing Tony's lifeless body, one of the revolutionaries says, "It's bad to die five minutes too soon." "No, Guillermo," China replies. "He's out there in the streets. The people are singing on his breath." Do not ask for whom the bell tolls . . . .

To sharpen the contrast with gay and splendid Havana, *We Were Strangers* sets political intrigue against tourist-brochure motifs. When China asks Tony why he has joined the Havana underground, he puts her off by spouting clichés: "I heard that rum was cheap and the girls were pretty and it was summer all year round." To the police he says that he has come to Havana to hire entertainers to bring back to the States. China corroborates his story by telling the police chief that Fenner has gone to the countryside to look for guajiro musicians. Even the dynamite sticks are smuggled inside a conga drum. But Fenner isn't a theatrical agent and he's not in the countryside scouting local talent. He's in the cellar of China's house digging a tunnel. And the conga drum is going to sound off with a different kind of bang. Cuba itself, the movie seems to say, is a conga drum stuffed with dynamite.

The villain in the movie is not Machado, whose name goes unmentioned, probably out of deference to Cuban and American sensibilities (Machado had died in Miami Beach ten years earlier), but the sinister Armando Ariete, played by the fine Mexican actor Pedro Armendáriz ("ariete" is Spanish for a battering ram), who is the head of Machado's feared secret police, La Porra ("porra" is Spanish for nightstick). In one of the movie's best scenes, he invites himself over for dinner at China's house. While the grime-covered revolutionaries cower in the cellar, Ariete chews on *moro* crabs, guzzles rum, and gives China a lecture on the excellence of Cuban men. Unlike Americans, who are incapable of true feeling, Cubans act out of sentiment, not self-interest (which does not mean, as he points out, that he wouldn't kill his own mother if she were found to be conspiring against El Presidente). Finally Ariete gets so drunk that he forgets his sense of honor and lunges at China. As he falls to the floor in a stupor, one of his henchmen drags him out of the house. (In Sylvester's novel, China is Ariete's illegitimate daughter, which adds a hint of incest to the encounter.)

A Latin Lover from hell, Ariete is Monte Blanca gone to rot. His charm is barely concealed savagery, his sentiments are no more than lust, and he is given to gambling—but with his own life, by playing Russian roulette. Latins not only make lousy lovers, as Helen Lawrenson asserted; they may be psychopaths as well. But more than a Latin Lover, Ariete is a "Cuban Heel," a phrase that merged early twentieth-century criminal slang with a punning reference to footwear. By the time Wini Shaw made fun of Jose O'Neill in *Melody for Two* (1937), the defining characteristics of the type were clear: dapper, well-mannered, charming, but utterly unprincipled. (In Shaw's song, "heel" rhymes with "kill.") This is how Andy Talbott, an American engineer in Coxe's *Murder in Havana*, describes Victor Guerra, "a slick-haired, smooth-talking Cuban heel": "He wore a suit of white silk-and-wool gabardine, faultlessly tailored, with a dark-red handkerchief popping from the breast pocket, and on his little finger was a good-sized star-sapphire. His teeth were startlingly white and perfect when he smiled and altogether Andy thought he was a pretty handsome guy—if you liked them smooth and Latin-looking."[5]

In spite of his grandiloquent name, Victor Guerra turns out to be a chump, but Ariete is a different story. Inside this caballero is a battering ram waiting to strike. With his angled panama hat, boutonniere, and gently accented baritone, he would cut a dashing figure, were it not for the submachine gun that he lugs around. Responsible for many murders, including that of China's brother, he brags about his victims like Don Juan counting conquests. Every night he puts Havana to bed, he says, by which he means that he patrols the streets until all the disturbances have been quashed.

The other Latin Lover in the movie, though a laconic and half-hearted one, is Fenner, whose real name is Antonio Luis Ferrer. Rather than a fake Latin, Tony is a fake American: ten years earlier he had fled Cuba with his father and has now returned to carry on the struggle. In nocturnal Havana nothing is what it seems. Punning on his official role, Ariete commends himself to China as "an authority on Havana nightlife." But the nightlife in the movie is nothing like *Week-End in Havana*'s. It's Ariete murdering dissenters, and Tony and four other men shoveling through human remains under the Colón cemetery. And the hopeful ending of the movie is no less deceptive, for the bright mañana—in Spanish the word means both "tomorrow" and "morning"—did not last. The years that followed Machado's overthrow were no less chaotic than those that preceded them. Between 1933 and 1936 Cuba had no fewer than eight presidents, and thousands of Cubans were forced into exile, among them thirteen-year-old Desi Arnaz and his father.

And then there is music, or rather the lack of it. The only song, untitled and uncredited, is performed by Gilbert Roland, who plays Guillermo, a dock worker with the heart of a troubadour. A one-man Greek chorus, Guillermo takes breaks from shoveling to comment on the action; the last few bars follow upon Fenner's death: "In 1933 Tony Fenner died for me. / Now I have one brother less, but I have my liberty." Sounding like a tune from

Rio Bravo or *The Man Who Shot Liberty Valance*, Guillermo's song—call it "The Ballad of Tony Fenner"—bears no relation to Cuban music. To make the difference unmistakable, Guillermo accompanies himself by softly strumming a guitar: no maracas or bongos or dancing feet. According to Tony, Havana is a place of "heat and crooked streets and fear and murder." As he says this, he is watching an ocean liner leave the harbor. In that ship goes bright Havana.[6]

During World War II, the influx of foreigners (real foreigners, not Americans) thickened Havana's noir atmosphere. A Caribbean Casablanca, the city was swarming with refugees, spies, and all kinds of shady characters, or so novelists and scriptwriters wanted you to believe. In *Murder in Havana*, the novel's hero discovers a Nazi spy ring that operates from U-boats stationed off the coast of Cuba. The Nazis photograph his secret plans for building a fleet of schooners, and in the course of chasing them he meets cash-starved aristocrats, concentration-camp survivors, corrupt politicians, and Rita Suárez, a Cuban seductress modeled on Rita Hayworth, then at the height of her fame. In the movie *The Bribe* (1949), a federal agent (Robert Taylor) travels to an island off the coast of Central America to stop the smuggling of airplane engines (in the Frederick Nebel story upon which the movie was based, the island is Cuba). He breaks up the ring and falls in love with sultry Elizabeth Hintten (Ava Gardner), an American ex-pat. In the novel *A Shot in the Dark* (1952), a World War II veteran tracks down his army buddy's murderer, the sinister Ranckosi, who turns out to be involved in human smuggling.

As in these instances, the basic plot idea in noir Havana fictions, cinematic or literary, repeats that of maraca musicals: put an American in Havana and watch him or her cope with the natives and their non-American ways. *A Lady without Passport* (1950), starring Hedi Lamarr and John Hodiak, opens with the murder of an undocumented Cuban immigrant on the streets of New York. Pretending to be a Hungarian refugee, immigration inspector Pete Karczag (Hodiak) goes to the island to investigate the traffic in illegal aliens. At the café where the Europeans hang out, he meets Marianne (Lamarr), a Viennese survivor of Buchenwald who is seeking passage to the States. Lovely Marianne becomes a vertex in the romantic triangle that pits American Pete against Palinov (George Macready), the self-described "Levantine" (like Joel Cairo in *The Maltese Falcon*) who heads the smuggling ring. When she finds out that Karczag is not who he says he is, she accepts Palinov's offer of passage to the United States.

Rife with echoes not only of *Casablanca* but of *Gilda* (where Macready, who specialized in playing refined villains, had a part similar to Palinov), *A Lady without Passport* stands apart less for its depiction of Havana than for its ambivalent portrayal of the United States. Unlike the heroes of similar stories, Karczag is not exactly a promoter of the American way of life. When Marianne tells him that she wants to come to the States, he warns her not to expect too much, for immigrants have dreams "with edges too round, colors too bright." Americans, he adds, tend to ostracize those who sound different or have a foreign last name (he should know). During the conversation, he and Marianne are strolling through Havana, a city full of displaced people, where all kinds of foreign accents float in the air. The implication that Cuba is more welcoming than the United States is hard to miss.

Karczag's ambivalence toward his homeland finds visual corroboration a few scenes later. Filmed partly on location, the Havana segments of the movie use atmospheric shots as much as any maraca musical. Daytime scenes take place along El Malecón, in the colonial plaza in front of the cathedral, against the backdrop of ships entering the harbor. Nighttime scenes make the most of smoke-filled bars and rumba parlors. Night or day, the narrow streets of Old Havana are teeming with life. Not so the scenes that take place in the United States. In the climactic last sequence, when Palinov is attempting to smuggle another load of Europeans (including Marianne) into the States, he is spotted by the American authorities. Flying over the Everglades, his plane runs out of gas and ditches into a river. Viewed from above, as Palinov searches for a place to land, the United States looks like a vast wilderness. Accustomed to Old World cities, one of the refugees says, "What kind of a country is this?" Shady characters notwithstanding, cosmopolitan Havana does seem a far more civilized place than America. *A Lady without Passport* opens with a killing on the streets of New York and ends with the luckless refugees stranded in a swamp. One can't help thinking that Marianne would have been better off staying in Cuba.

In the 1950s, noir Havana resurfaced in a radio series that, despite the fame of its leading actors, is remembered today only by cultists of Golden Age Radio. When Hemingway's *To Have and Have Not* was turned into a movie in 1944, the setting was moved to Martinique and the anti-Machado revolutionaries were reborn as anti-Vichy freedom fighters. These changes occurred in response to pressure from the Office of the Coordinator of Inter-American Affairs, which did not want to offend Fulgencio Batista, at the time Cuba's democratically elected president and an ally of the United States. Several years later, however, Bogart and Bacall would have the opportunity to reprise their movie roles in their original setting. Recorded in 1951 and 1952, the serial *Bold Venture* began airing nationally in the spring of 1951, eventually running on more than four hundred radio stations. Seventy-eight episodes were produced, though only about half of them seem to have survived. Bogart plays Slate Shannon, the owner of a charter boat, *The Bold Venture*, and a quasi-respectable hotel, Shannon's Place. Bacall is Vassar-educated Sailor Duvall, whose late father was Shannon's friend.

Although Warner Brothers vetted the scripts to ensure that the program did not poach too much on *To Have and Have Not*, the audit had little effect, for the characters in the radio series are nearly identical to those in the movie. Slate is the cynical tough guy with a sentimental streak—a lonely man with delusions of mayhem, as he is described in one episode. Sailor is his kittenish sidekick, forever baiting him with sexual innuendo. Slate usually takes the bait:

> Sailor: You talk about Havana like it was a woman.
> Slate: Do I?
> Sailor: How do you talk about me behind my back?
> Slate: Walk ahead of me and I'll think of something.

The regular characters also include Slate's Haitian factotum, King Moses (Jester Hairston), who provides transitions between scenes by recapping the plot in calypso songs (somewhere along the way, *Casablanca's* Sam got rerouted to Port-au-Prince and acquired a West Indian accent), and Inspector LaSalle, a Cuban cop with a French name (shades of Captain Renault) and a gift for malapropisms: "With such a bird in my hand, why should I go beating up bushes?"

No less familiar than the characters is the locale, "the sultry setting of tropical Havana and the mysterious islands of the Caribbean." In the episodes that unfold on the mysterious islands, Slate and Sailor run into modern-day pirates, witch doctors, natives who sling poisoned darts. When Slate and Sailor stick to dark Havana, the fare is mystery rather than mysterious: Cuban revolutionaries smuggling guns; hoods impersonating honeymooners; trophy wives plotting to murder their sugar daddies (usually also sugar barons). Add to the mix priceless statuettes from China, jade from Burma, opium from Macao, sapphires from India—and the result is a menu of noir motifs. Regardless of the plot, however, Slate and Sailor keep coming across dead bodies, made that way not only by guns and knives but by horses, gamecocks, and X-ray machines. So many shots and shouts ring out in each episode that it's difficult to keep track of the victims. Whenever the scriptwriters seem to run out of flirtatious repartee for Bogie and Bacall, they drop a corpse in one of the rooms of Shannon's Place, "Murder Hotel," as LaSalle calls it. "What is it about us," Slate says to Sailor, "that always makes us eye-witnesses to people's dying?" No wonder that the talisman of their romance is a .25-caliber Colt, "our song, that little souvenir of blue steel."

The patrons of Shannon's Place are not so different from those who frequent Rick's Café, its model. As in Casablanca, everyone is looking for something or has something to hide. When the occasional tourists stray in, they wander around in a daze, as if they too were displaced people looking for a letter of transit. Although they may come only for a weekend, often they never make it back. (In noir Havana time also stands still.) In *A Lady without Passport*, a French resident of the city remarks: "Here you can see everything." In *Bold Venture*, Slate says: "There's a little bit of everywhere in Havana." These phrases define the city's cosmopolitanism, its receptiveness to strangers, a trait that goes back to the eighteenth century, when the British occupation opened the harbor to the world. Two centuries later, in *Bold Venture* and *A Lady without Passport*, the city is once again occupied by European invaders, the victims of war rather than its perpetrators.

One of the last Hollywood films shot in Cuba before the Castro revolution, *The Big Boodle* (1957) represents the culmination, and in some sense the unraveling, of noir Havana. Based on another Robert Sylvester novel, the film descends from *We Were Strangers*, since some of the main characters are relatives of Tony Fenner. Instead of a people's struggle for freedom, however, the subject here is one man's efforts to keep himself out of harm's way. The movie stars a jowly, somber Errol Flynn, looking nothing like the dashing swashbuckler of *Captain Blood*, the role that had made him famous twenty years earlier. Flynn plays Ned Sherwood (his last name a reminder of another of Flynn's defining roles), a blackjack dealer inadvertently involved in a scheme to circulate three million counterfeit pesos, the "big boodle." Suspected both by the crooks and the cops—in the person of Colonel Mastegui, the Havana police chief, once again played with gusto by Pedro Armendáriz—Sherwood is beaten up, run over, stabbed, tied up, shot at. Although he hardly seems to have the energy for it, he gets tangled up romantically with the two beautiful daughters (one good, one bad) of the president of Cuba's national bank, Armando Ferrer, who worries that the phony bills will tarnish Cuba's "good government," headed by none other than Fulgencio Batista, who had come to power in a coup a few years earlier. Señor Ferrer's son, who died fighting the Machado dictatorship, is none other than Antonio Luis Ferrer, a.k.a. Tony Fenner.

A noir in broad daylight, the movie transpires almost entirely under the harsh Havana sun. When Mastegui's agents stop tailing Sherwood, he becomes "a decoy without a shadow," a description that applies to the movie's style, which dispenses with the chiaroscuros typical of the genre. Even the scene at the casino during which Flynn is passed the counterfeit pesos occurs, somewhat improbably, in the middle of the day. Although *The Big Boodle* is a kind of sequel to *We Were Strangers*, cinematically the two movies could not be more different. Subterranean Havana has given way to a locale of ruthless exposure, a tropical panopticon where only the big boodle remains invisible, though not for long. In *We Were Strangers*, China's brother believes that the city will shelter him from Ariete's goons: "Havana takes care of her own. She will hide me." Although he is gunned down a few moments later, Tony Fenner and his companions make clear that it is indeed possible to go underground in Havana. But not so in the city of *The Big Boodle*, Sherwood's treeless forest, which, unlike its venerable predecessor, offers no hiding places. Pursued by the counterfeiters, Sherwood becomes "a cream puff in the sun," a metaphor of vulnerability whose physical expression is his tanned but battered face.

Still, the brightness is misleading, no less counterfeit than the phony bills. That the Cuban underworld operates in the light of day does not make its schemes more transparent. For its British release, the title of the film was changed to "Night in Havana," incongruous if one thinks of the film's lighting, but accurate as an allusion to the cycle of violence in which Sherwood is snared. As "the zombie behind the blackjack table," he stalks the city in search of clues, which allows Havana landmarks—from El Malecón to the jai alai frontón—to pass before the viewer. It comes as no surprise, then, that the climactic scene takes place in the Morro Castle, where the plates for the counterfeit pesos are hidden. In what amounts to a last tribute to his screen persona, Flynn storms a castle as he did in *Robin Hood*, except that he is taken there by a ferry boat. As a tour guide leads tourists around El Morro, pointing out that it was built to defend the city from English pirates (like Captain Blood), Sherwood comes upon the counterfeiter on the sun-drenched esplanade at the top of the fortress, with its rows of rusted Spanish cannons. Flabby though he is, Sherwood has no trouble getting the best of the bad guy, who falls off the parapet into the shark-infested waters. As the movie ends, he and the good Ferrer daughter (Fina, rhymes with China) stroll arm in arm into the sunlight.

Released three years after *The Big Boodle*, Errol Flynn's last film would be *Cuban Rebel Girls* (1959). Done in semidocumentary style, it finds Flynn, who plays himself, joining forces with Fidel Castro to topple the same good government praised in *The Big Boodle.* He is aided by sixteen-year-old Beverly Aadland, at the time Flynn's real-life paramour. Although *Cuban Rebel Girls* is an embarrassment, artistically as well as politically, it ushered in a new era in American perceptions of Cuba. For the next fifty years, when Americans thought of Cuba, they would think not only of the rumba and the mambo, Ricky and Lucy, or bright and noir Havana, but also of the bearded revolutionaries that Flynn befriended in a last attempt to rehabilitate his fading career. Whether festive or mournful, bolero time would be no more. It was now time for the revolution.

SEVEN

Comic Comandantes, Exotic Exiles

Me, I always tell the truth. Even when I lie.
—Tony Montana in *Scarface* (1983)

Americans went to Cuba first as travelers, then as soldiers, then as tourists. And then, fifty years ago, they stopped going. Fulgencio Batista had been a friendly dictator; Fidel Castro turned out to be a most unfriendly one. In April 1961, a year after the last broadcast of the *Lucy-Desi Comedy Hour*, the failed Bay of Pigs invasion damaged beyond repair the shaky relations between the United States and the regime that had come to power two years earlier. A few months after the invasion, the Kennedy administration imposed an embargo on Cuban goods and restrictions on travel to the island. No longer America's best good neighbor, Cuba became its closest enemy. The Havana born in 1919 with the Eighteenth Amendment perished forty years later with another type of prohibition.

As the seat of a communist regime with rabidly anti-American leaders, Cuba moved from the back of America's mind to the front pages of its newspapers. Although geopolitical considerations had always been a part of American thinking about Cuba, during the first half of the twentieth century the island's turbulent politics had few repercussions in the United States. Cuban presidents came and went (usually to exile in America), revolts broke out and subsided, the economy surged and sank according to world sugar prices—and through it all the tourists kept coming. Cuban politicians, whatever their ideology, did their best to reassure their northern neighbors that, regardless of local politics, the conditions for visitors remained propitious. In the early thirties, when opposition to the Machado dictatorship was as its height, Havana's mayor and other officials constantly reminded Americans that the city was safe and welcoming. If anything, Cuban politics provided more material for Latin-themed entertainment, as in "Revolt in Cuba," a dance number from Irving Berlin's *As Thousands Cheer* (1933) inspired by Machado's overthrow.

Beginning in 1959, however, pleasure island became "Revolutionary Cuba," with the adjective marking the break between past and present. Cuba had had revolutions before, of course, but not like this one, which not only transformed the island's government and economy but sent hundreds of thousands of its citizens into exile. For the first time since the Spanish-American War, Cuba did not evoke rumba numbas or holidays in Havana, but missiles and refugees. In a 1969 episode of the TV series *I Dream of Jeannie*, Jeannie's husband, an air force pilot, lands in Havana by mistake. Although the title of the episode is "I'll See You in C-U-B-A," the Cuba we see is no longer the rum hounds' paradise of the 1920s. Captain Nelson is captured by fatigue-clad revolutionaries who cannot understand what he is doing there, since "nobody ever comes to Cuba voluntarily." Only Jeannie's magical powers, exercised while cha-cha music plays in the background, are able to spirit him out.

The Cuban Revolution yielded two iconic figures, each recognizable by first name or nickname alone: Fidel and Che. Although they burst on the American imagination with the glitter of the new, their American personas drew on an old stereotype, that of the Latin Lover, who now enhanced his erotic appeal with revolutionary mystique. Instead of neat mustaches, scraggly beards. Instead of dinner jackets, army fatigues. Instead of daiquiris, Molotov cocktails. The corny title of a novel by the Cuban Manuel Cofiño López sums up the makeup of the Guerrilla Lover: *La última mujer y el próximo combate*—"The last woman and the next battle." In *We Were Strangers*, Armando Ariete also went for women and guns, but he was on the side of the oppressors. Liberators rather than scourges—or so many thought—Che and Fidel were on the side of the oppressed.

Their specific identities differed, however. Argentinean Che—handsome, heroic, inscrutable—descended from Fernando Lamas; Cuban Fidel—paunchy, garrulous, histrionic—from Cesar Romero. If Che possessed animal magnetism, Fidel had bilongo.

Alberto Korda's legendary photograph of Che Guevara, one of the most reproduced images in the world, gracing (or disgracing) everything from tea cups to T-shirts, shows an intense young man peering into the distance. His beret, worn at an angle, gives him a bohemian, almost an artistic air; but his cold stare is implacable. This man is a visionary, at the very least a zealot. Obstruct his dream of global revolution at your peril. In contrast, a 1960 *New York Times* cartoon pictures a hapless Fidel attempting to make a Cuba Libre without Coke (fig. 12). Uncle Sam offers a helping hand—the paradoxical implication is that without U.S. assistance Cuba cannot be "libre"—but Fidel has his back turned. The empty bottles on the floor testify to his stubbornness. He will keep trying to concoct Cokeless rum-and-Cokes, even if in the process he uses up all of the rum on the island. Another cartoon shows a bumbling Fidel inadvertently slipping into Russian during one of his speeches: "Cuba Si, Yanki Nyet!—Oops" (fig. 13). In the background Che smiles, seemingly pleased by Fidel's slip.

In *Che!* (1969), the first—and worst—of several hagiographic films about the Argentine, these differences are already clear. Although the reality was more complicated, in the movie Che is the revolution's real leader, the power behind the podium. He plans the military campaigns, feeds Fidel lines for his speeches, oversees Cuba's economy as well as its firing squads. Infantile and hedonistic, Fidel swills Metaxa and puffs on a cigar. After Batista has fled, while Che works in his Spartan room at La Cabaña

'CUBA LIBRE'

Lukas in La Union, Valparaiso, Chile

"It's difficult without the coke."

Fig. 12. "Cuba Libre." Cartoon by Renzo Pecchenino (Lukas). *New York Times*, January 31, 1960. Courtesy Fundación Lukas, Valparaiso, Chile.

"Cuba Si, Yanqui Nyet! — Oops —"

Fig. 13. "Cuba Si, Yanki Nyet!" *Washington Post*, April 6, 1961. A 1961 Herblock Cartoon, copyright by the Herb Block Foundation.

fortress, Fidel has a party in the penthouse of a swank Havana hotel. When the two of them have a falling out, Fidel grabs a bottle of brandy, screams for his mistress, and locks himself in his suite. Che goes off to Bolivia to continue the revolution. Unhappy with the original script, Jack Palance, who played Fidel, asked for changes so that his character would appear less "buffoonish."[1] If the changes were made, they didn't change much. Che is the hero; Fidel, the entertaining sidekick.

Although a man who managed to stay in power for half a century—longer than any other Latin American dictator—is hardly a buffoon, the ironic view of Fidel stuck. Perhaps it was his loquacity, foreign to a culture that prizes tight lips, or his ever-present boots and fatigues, laughable to a people whose political leaders wear business suits, or his humorlessness, unusual in a Cuban, or his over-the-top tirades against the United States—whatever the reasons, Fidel personified the Cuban Revolution as comic relief.

In *Up the Sandbox* (1972), Margaret, a bored young housewife (Barbra Streisand), fantasizes that she attends a speech by Fidel in a New York hotel. After she challenges his machismo during the question-and-answer session, she is invited up to his room. He plies her with wine and they dance a mambo. Suddenly Fidel rips off his beard. Startled, Margaret wants to leave, but he chases her onto the sofa, where he tears open his shirt to reveal his great secret: breasts. The comandante is really a "womandante," as if César Romero were a cross-dressed Carmen Miranda. In the Anne Richardson Roiphe novel that inspired the movie, when Margaret snaps out of her fantasy, she says to herself: "Secretly I know that part of me would remain forever faithful to Fidel."[2] But the Fidel who inspires fidelity is not the heroic rebel leader, but the one who, in every sense, lacks *cojones*.

If *Up the Sandbox* re-genders Fidel as Fidelle, in *Bananas* (1971) the transformation is even more astounding: he is reborn as Woody Allen. Another send-up of the Cuban Revolution, the movie takes Fielding Mellish (Allen) to the mythical republic of San Marcos, where a Fidel look-alike (Jacobo Morales, the same Puerto Rican actor who played Fidel in *Up the Sandbox*) topples the military dictator, but becomes so drunk with power that he makes Swedish the country's official language. The guerrilla leader is deposed and Fielding becomes top banana. Donning a red beard, he travels to the United States, where Fielding-Fidel at long last manages to bed his activist girlfriend, who is thrilled to be making love to the charismatic comandante, a Latin Lover for the politically progressive. In Allen's view, a banana republic is one whose leaders, whether of the right or the left or Manhattan, are all bananas.

This is not to say, however, that the flesh-and-blood Fidel has not had more than his share of admirers. What the playwright Mel Arrighi called the "Castro Complex"—an irrational infatuation that, in Arrighi's play, leads the protagonist to ask her husband to put on a beard and fatigues before they have sex—has claimed many victims. Fidel first came to the attention of Americans in a series of articles by Herbert Matthews, a veteran reporter who had also covered the Spanish Civil War. After an all-night car trip from Havana to the Sierra Maestra, Matthews met with Fidel early in 1957, less than a year after he had landed in Cuba to mount an armed insurrection against the Batista regime. Castro opened a box of cigars to mark the occasion and proceeded to talk, with little interruption, for three hours. The journalist's first impression: "This was quite a man—a powerful six-footer, olive-skinned, full-faced, with a scraggly beard. . . . Here was an educated, dedicated fanatic, a man of ideals, of courage and of remarkable qualities of leadership." Subsequent stories by Matthews, who later claimed that he had "invented" Fidel, elaborated on the charisma of "the most remarkable and romantic figure to arise in Cuban history since José Martí, the hero of the wars of independence."[3]

After Matthews's pieces in the *New York Times*, appraisals of Castro as a romantic revolutionary appeared with regularity in the American press. For some, he was a bearded Robin Hood, taking from the rich to give to the poor; others, even more stricken with the Castro Complex, regarded him as a messiah, and not just for Cuba but for all of Latin America. Norman Mailer, who likened Fidel to the ghost of Hernán Cortés riding Emiliano Zapata's white horse, regarded him as "the first and greatest hero to appear in the world since the second world war." In April 1959, when Castro spoke in New York to the Women Lawyers Association, he was met with "fluttery glances" from the audience, one attendee likening him to a "younger Jimmy Stewart." Abbie Hoffman's account of Fidel's triumphant entrance into Havana resorts to a different term of comparison: "The tank stops in the city square. Fidel lets the gun drop to the ground, slaps his thigh and stands erect. He is like a mighty penis coming to life, and when he is tall and straight, the crowd is immediately transformed"—into what, Hoffman does not say, but we can guess.[4]

In *A Race of Rebels* (1960), an early novel about the revolution, the narrator describes Castro as a man with "a knightly aura," "an authentic hero who would not have looked silly wearing a crimson cloak and riding a white charger." He goes on to say that Fidel could have been Richard the Lion-Hearted or George Washington. The opening scene of Cristina García's *Dreaming in Cuban* (1992) has the protagonist's Cuban grandmother fantasizing about being ravished by El Líder himself on a red velvet divan. In Mary Morris's *House Arrest* (1996), about an American writer who helps Fidel's illegitimate daughter escape the island, Castro is a Don Juan who has engendered children all over the island. "¡Qué cojones!" says one of his admirers, "Our leader never sleeps in the same bed two nights in a row." In Stephen Hunter's thriller, *Havana* (2003), Fidel in bed is "magnificent, a tiger, an athlete again." "What a man you are!" exclaims one of his lovers, exhausted, as Fidel leans back on the bed and lights a cigar.[5]

Whether intended as fiction or not, it is difficult to read these effusions today with a straight face. Filmmaker Saul Landau, a long-time apologist for the Cuban Revolution, believes that Castro has a "religious aura" about him. Nonetheless, one man's aura is another man's dialogue bubble, and for as long as he has been around—and he has been around a long time—Fidel has inspired ridicule as well as reverence, even among many Cubans on both sides of the Florida Straits, to whom he is "Fifo." A few years ago, when a mysterious illness incapacitated him, the joke was that he was now a "coma-andante," a walking coma. When he handed the reins of power to his brother Raúl, who isn't much younger, Slate.com pictured them side by side in wheelchairs, next to an IV bag labeled "Cuba." The caption: "The tube has been passed" (fig. 14). Already back in 1968, a survey of world leaders listed the charismatic (the Kennedys, Mao, Che) and noncharismatic (the Nixons, Lester Maddox, Raúl Castro). Fidel was the only figure who appeared on both lists: as young rebel, charismatic; as middle-aged demagogue, uncharismatic.[6] Unlike Che, a murderer held up as a martyr, Fidel is a dictator held up as a clown.

The comic comandante was not the only stock character to emerge from the Cuban Revolution. Within ten years of Castro's coming to power, about half a million Cubans—10 percent of the island's population at the time—elected to leave the country, most of them settling in South Florida. In the decades since, several hundred thousand more have followed. Because the initial waves of exiles were predominantly white and middle-class, and because they came to this country as political refugees, they stood apart from other Latinos. Economically savvy but politi-

Fig. 14. "The Tube Has Been Passed." Cartoon by Glenn McCoy. Glenn McCoy © 2008 *Belleville News-Democrat*. Dist. by Universal Uclick. Reprinted with permission. All rights reserved.

cally zany, Cuban exiles were different. They were just as likely to set off a bomb as to start a business. After a car bomb goes off in Miami, a character in Edna Buchanan's *Act of Betrayal* (1996) says: "Hope all that Cuban crap ain't starting up again."[7] Cuban crap: bombs in Little Havana, paramilitary camps in the Everglades, cocaine cowboys in cigarette boats, excitable exiles plotting over cups of espresso—the stuff of the TV series *Miami Vice*, *CSI Miami*, and the short-lived *Cane*.

Or of *Scarface*. Panned when it first appeared but now a cult favorite among Americans and Cuban Americans alike, Brian De

Palma's 1983 remake of the classic 1932 mob movie produced the best-known U.S. Cuban after Ricky Ricardo: Tony Montana, the ultimate Cuban Heel, the star of video games, comic books, and gangsta-rap lyrics. In De Palma's movie, Tony (Al Pacino) arrives in the Mariel Boatlift of 1980 and quickly becomes the kingpin of the thriving South Florida drug trade. Ruthless, he thinks nothing of murdering those he considers "cocoroaches," a category that includes some associates, most competitors, and all communists. This heel has a soft spot for family ties, though, which makes him call off a hit to protect the target's wife and daughters. In revenge, the Bolivians who ordered the murder go after him. In the spectacular last scene, a bullet-riddled Tony plunges into the reflecting pool in his foyer to the hieratic strains of organ music. As he floats face down in the bloodied water, the camera pans up to a sculpture of several naked nymphs in a circle (a reminiscence of the Gran Casino Nacional fountain?) holding up a globe with his slogan: "The world is yours."

Just as Armando Ariete is Cesar Romero gone bad, Tony Montana is Ricky Ricardo's evil twin, his life an enactment of the American dream as xenophobic nightmare. Like Ricky, Tony leaves Cuba, marries a sexy American (Michelle Pfeiffer), and in his own way becomes a success. But that's where the resemblance ends. The American emcee at the disco where Tony hangs out, the Babylon Club, does an imitation of Ricky Ricardo, the "favorite Cuban of all time." While the emcee is impersonating Ricky, the camera pans the audience and captures Tony sprawled in one of the booths, sipping a drink and looking blankly toward the stage. The message is clear: the iconic Cuban used to be Ricky Ricardo, the nightclub performer, and now it is Tony Montana, the drug dealer. This is why the nightclub's name—Babylon—echoes Ricky's—Babalú. But Babalú was a place for wholesome Latin-themed entertainment (even little Ricky performed at his father's club), while the Babylon is a disco-driven den for cokeheads.

If the Babylon is a decadent Babalú, Tony's marriage to Elvie is a grotesque version of Lucy and Ricky's. Almost as violent as any murder, Tony and Elvie's venomous exchanges have nothing in common with the Ricardos' hilarious quarrels. Unlike Ricky and Lucy, Tony and Elvie don't have any children because, Tony says, Elvie's womb has been "polluted" by drugs. And in Elvie's eyes Tony is not a Cuban dreamboat but a "spic millionaire." Instead of the heart on satin, the emblem of their marriage is the heap of cocaine on Elvie's dressing table.

And then there is Tony's accent, on which Pacino apparently worked very hard. Not even Ricky at his most hysterical sounded anything like Tony, who speaks as if his mouth had been stuffed with cotton. When Ricky gets angry, he occasionally allows himself a Spanish cussword, but Tony's speech is a babbling brook of obscenities, particularly—as Elvie complains—the all-purpose "fock" and its variants. At the time the movie was released, Miami Cubans vociferously protested its portrayal of exiles, but *Scarface* is no more offensive than *Cuban Pete* or *Weekend in Ha-*

vana, and not because of the disclaimer at the end, but because it's hard to take Tony seriously.[8] Montana may rhyme with Havana, but no *habaneros* would ever confuse him with one of their own.

Partly because most of the scenes could not be filmed in Miami (that Cuban crap again—bomb threats), and partly because of Giorgio Moroder's score, which is strong on synthesizer and weak on maracas, *Scarface* depends mostly on Manny Ribera, Tony's best friend, his *monina*, for atmospheric effects. Played by Havana-born Steven Bauer, who in the 1970s had starred in *Qué pasa U.S.A.?* a bilingual PBS sitcom about three generations of an exile family, Manny fills every scene that he's in with Spanglish patter. When Tony makes a nasty remark about Elvie's former lover, many years her senior, Bauer adlibs: "Cuidado que no te pase a ti, se te cae" (Watch out, you might not get it up either). Tony's banker wants to charge him more for laundering money, and Manny interrupts: "Mira, olvídate, we go somewhere else, ok?" In the funniest scene in the movie, Manny teaches Tony to pick up *americanas* the Cuban way—by flicking his tongue at them, a gesture that Tony (less Cuban than he seems) finds "disgusting." The script by Oliver Stone has Manny remark about a girl in a bikini, "Hey, look at the chick, huh?" On the screen Bauer translates the line into: "Mira eso, men, mira esa jeva, men!" To which his buddy Chi-Chi (Ángel Salazar) retorts in Cuban kind: "¡Coño, qué rica!"

Nothing exceeds like excess, says Elvie in one of *Scarface's* most quoted lines. She could also have said: nothing exceeds like exiles, since the *marielito* criminals easily outdo their Italian-American precursors in savagery and glitz. The original Scarface, Tony Camonte, lives in a gaudy apartment with reinforced doors and bullet-proof shutters—a "steel fort." But it's nothing compared to Tony Montana's walled palazzo, complete with pet tiger, a state-of-the art surveillance system and dozens of armed guards. For the final shoot-out, De Palma stages a scene that resembles a Latin American coup more than a gangster flick. As an army of guerrillas invades Tony's compound, he goes to an armoire and takes out an assault rifle mounted with a grenade launcher, "the little friend" with which he says hello to the intruders, blasting away from the top of the grand marble staircase. In the original *Scarface*, the police encircle Tony's apartment and he is shot in the back when he tries to escape. In De Palma's remake, Tony dies in a blaze of gore and gunfire.

Though she has not become a folk hero like Tony Montana, Dorita Pérez, the *marielita* protagonist of *The Perez Family* (1995), completes and, to some extent, corrects the Hollywood depiction of the Cuban exile. In the Christine Bell novel on which the movie is based, forty-four-year-old Dorita Perez is fifty pounds overweight "on the Anglo scale" but perfect "on the Latin scale."[9] In the movie, Dorita (Marisa Tomei) is twenty years younger and fifty pounds lighter (Hollywood applies the Anglo scale). The cinematic Dorita also has a different profession. In the novel she is mistaken for a prostitute; in the movie there is no mistake: she is a whore, and not just any whore, but a symbolic one: "I am Cuba, used by many, conquered by no one. I am siempre *la isla*." When she is asked why she wants to leave Cuba, she replies: "I want to fuck John Wayne." When she finds out that John Wayne is dead, she weeps inconsolably. It seems that on the Anglo scale Cuba stacks up as a voluptuous, free-spirited *jinetera* with a hankering for American men.

Desperate to get out of the detention camp for Mariel refugees, Tony Montana agrees to murder a former Castro sympathizer. Dorita takes a different approach: she contrives a family. Since families have a better chance than individuals of finding a sponsor, and since she is a "Pérez," as common a last name in Cuba as Smith or Jones in the United States, it doesn't take her long to recruit three other Pérezes to pass as relatives: Juan, a former political prisoner whose wife, Carmela, has been waiting for him in Miami; Papi, a crazy old man who runs around naked and climbs trees; and Felipe, an orphaned teenager who survives by selling sundries from a shopping cart. Sponsored by the Church of the Resurrection, they leave the Orange Bowl and move into the rectory. While Dorita looks after her newly founded family, Juan renews his search for Carmela, but when they finally find each other, after several near misses, they decide to go their separate ways: she, toward Officer Pirelli, a federal agent who investigated a break-in at her house; he, back to Dorita. As the Cuban-born Pérez family withers, the American-born Perez family takes root. By the end, all three protagonists—Dorita, Juan, Carmela—have severed their ties with the past.

Exile has turned them into other people. Dorita the harlot has been resurrected as Dottie the matriarch; Juan, who used to own a sugar cane plantation, now sells flowers on street corners; and Carmela, for two decades an inert Penelope, has fallen in love with a suitor. Even Officer Pirelli, a northerner stationed temporarily in Miami, decides to stay on and start a new career.

What's odd is that the songs that accompany almost every scene don't reflect the changes in the characters. Outside of a brief disco number, all of them date back to pre-Castro Cuba. At the Key West dock where Dorita disembarks, a couple of old men with guitars appear out of nowhere singing "Amor de mi bohío," a 1935 son in praise of rustic life in Cuba. In her quaint Coral Gables home, Carmela takes a bubble bath listening to the opening bars of *La engañadora*, the song that started the chachachá craze in 1951. When Dorita and Juan make love, an Afro-Cuban lullaby plays in the background. The movie's theme, "Mata siguaraya," interpreted by the legendary sonero Beny Moré, speaks about a native tree—the "siguaraya"—that cannot be felled without permission from the *orishas*, the gods. It is a song about continuity, about tradition, about respect for the homegrown. Either "Mata siguaraya" doesn't apply to family trees, or exile is more powerful than the orishas, for it rends asunder what Cuba joined together.

And so, even as *The Perez Family* propels the characters into the future, toward new lives and identities, it insists on the world they left behind. Like Cuban exiles themselves, the movie looks backward and forward at the same time. In the last line, Juan says about Papi, his factitious father, who is perched atop a palm tree, "Always he is looking for Cuba." As Juan speaks the line, Moré begins to sing "Mata siguaraya" and the screen fills up with an aerial shot of an ocean, a beach, and finally a lush, tropical landscape, where palms and siguarayas abound. It is as if we were traveling to Cuba on the wings of the old man's imagination. Strangely, this "coming to America" movie ends where it began, in the country the characters left to come to America. Although Papi doesn't speak a single word (exile has silenced him), he is the movie's sentient center, to use Henry James's phrase, the character who defines tone and sensibility. In Christine Bell's novel, Papi is accidentally killed—an obvious sign that the past is no longer relevant. Directed by Mira Nair, herself foreign-born, the movie is more probing in its recognition of the contradictory allegiances of the exile. Though mute, Papi speaks for all those Cubans who have refused to let go of their homeland even after abandoning it. (The actor who plays Papi is Lázaro Pérez—not only the one Cuban among the major players, but the one true Pérez.)

The place where Dorita and Juan become new people—and where crazy Papi refuses to do so—is Miami, the magic city, the preserve of exotic exiles and other wildlife. Usually portrayed as a frontier town between Anglo and Latin America, a combination Dodge City and Casablanca, Cuban-overrun Miami—Little Havana for short—has also seized the American imagination.

(Some years ago, local officials were happy to capitalize on the city's disrepute with the slogan: Miami, the rules are different here.) Two conceits recur in descriptions of contemporary Miami. The first is that it is dreamlike, a chimera of shiny surfaces and pastel shades. An American newspaperman in Gail Godwin's novel *Queen of the Underworld* (2006) puts it this way: "Miami is not like anywhere on earth. That's why I love it, it's surreal." Normally measured, Joan Didion describes the city in language that could have been lifted from *Havana Mañana:* "Miami seemed not a city at all but a tale, a romance of the tropics, a kind of waking dream."[10]

In fact, any time Didion travels to Miami, not an American city but "a settlement of considerable interest," she experiences a zero-gravity moment, as if she were traveling to another planet: "I never passed through security for a flight to Miami without experiencing a certain weightlessness, the heightened wariness of having left the developed world for a more fluid atmosphere." The familiar distinction between place and atmosphere recurs here to express the distinctiveness—and the backwardness—not of Cuba but of its northern outpost. According to Didion, this "atmospheric anomaly" gives the city the feel of make-believe, a locale where appearances deceive and nothing seems fixed (even the way Cubans soften consonants, she says, contributes to the impression of fluidity). Writing in *Vanity Fair,* Jan Morris has the same impression, but couches it in less flattering, more flattening, imagery: "[Miami] is like a vast jelly, flattened by some kitchen catastrophe and squashed out of all recognizable mold." What Havana was to James Steele or Waldo Frank, Miami is to Morris and Didion. In their accounts, solidity and boundaries define civilized life, if not reality itself. An amorphous settlement, a city without city limits, tends to unreality, barbarism, or comparisons with extraterrestrial life. Morris's "vast jelly" is reminiscent of nothing so much as of the alien "blob" of science-fiction fame. When she wonders what will become of Miami, she jokes—but is it only a joke?—that maybe "the Cubans" will use it as "a base for the domination of the USA."[11] "Beware the Blob," the theme song of *The Blob* (1958), may well be the message here.

The other—related—conceit is that Miami is not only a Little Havana but Havana in reverse, its mirror image. Instead of hard left, hard right; instead of Marxist slogans, designer labels; instead of sugar cane, cocaine. Cuban-American novelist Carolina García-Aguilera has one of her characters sum up the similarities: "Neither side allowed free thinking, free discourse. Both sides punished those who stepped out of line, both through social ostracism and physical violence."[12] In Buchanan's *Act of Betrayal*, the protagonist dreams that everybody in Miami is named Raúl—as in Raúl Castro. In *Scarface*, the immigration official who interviews Tony Montana believes that by sending people like Tony to the United States, "Castro is shitting on us." Miami: the dumping ground for Cuban refuse.

In the early months of 2000, the saga of Elian González, a seven-year-old boy whose mother drowned in the Florida Straits trying to come to the United States, hardened these antiexile views. When Elián's Miami relatives, understandably, refused to give him up to the immigration authorities for repatriation, American journalists and pundits could not contain their outrage. In the *New York Times*, Bob Herbert wondered why the authorities had not dealt with the "crazies" who were holding Elián. *Washington Post* columnist Judy Mann blamed the "insanity" of Miami Cubans for "poisoning American-Cuban relations ever since Mr. Castro took over." *Time* magazine opined that expatriate Cubans had fled a totalitarian state only to set up a "satellite version" across the Florida Straits. Others joked that Dade County was the only American municipality with a foreign policy. Even David Rieff, who had written sympathetically about exiles in *Going to Miami* (1987) and *The Exile* (1993), chimed in that the city had turned into "an out-of-control banana republic within the American body politic."[13]

Since the early 1990s, the perception of Cuban exiles as fiery exotics, crazies with a cause, has gone hand in hand with a renewed interest in mainland Cuba. After the demise of the Soviet Union, with the island's economy on the brink of collapse, the Castro regime resorted to tourism to compensate for the loss of Soviet subsidies. Cuba once again became, in the words of brochures, "the hippest island in the world," the mecca of rumba revelers and cigar aficionados. Although travel restrictions were—and are—still in place, many Americans managed to visit the island. Every year hundreds of American college students enrolled in "study abroad" programs that advertised Cuba with such slogans as "¡Cuba Sí!" (one half of the Castroite motto: "¡Cuba sí, Yankis, no!") or "Once forbidden, now essential, feel the warmth!" One university was not above alluding discreetly to the Cuban sex trade with the promise of "cruising the streets in 1950s cars."[14] Those too old for study abroad reached Cuba from Canada, Mexico, or the Bahamas and came back with a few smuggled cigars and a suntan. Still others enjoyed the island's charms the way most Americans always had, vicariously, through photographs of Old Havana and young Havanans.

Revolutionary Cuba's appeal lay not only in its beaches and its weather, but in the remnants and revivals of prerevolutionary Cuba: antique American cars; restored colonial buildings; tunes like "Siboney" and "Mamá Inés" interpreted by senescent soneros; and the ubiquitous prostitutes or jineteras. About the last, the Web site sexincuba.com remarked that, in Cuba, "There may not be freedom of speech but there certainly is freedom of sex."[15] Ironically, Castro's Cuba seemed to be a marketable commodity to the extent that it reminded Americans of the country that existed before Castro took over. Indeed, it is striking how many of the Cuban-themed movies of the last fifty years look back to pre-Castro Havana, the sexiest city in the world: *Godfather II* (1974), *Cuba* (1979), *Havana* (1990), *The Mambo Kings* (1992), *Dirty Dancing: Havana Nights* (2004), *The Lost City* (2005). More than half a century later, Americans continue to be fascinated by their island paradise of rum, rump, and rumba.

Stereotypes die hard, if at all. In the 1980s, Gloria Estefan became famous doing the conga, exactly as Desi Arnaz had done fifty years earlier. In the 1990s, Francine Prose described Miami as if it were the stage set of a 1940s musical: "One feels the spirit of Carmen Miranda hovering over the new Miami, informing and reflecting the city's sense of itself: flashy, Latin, exotic, dangerous and sexy, self-mocking and ironically self-obsessed."[16] Even when the setting is realistic, as in *The Perez Family*, the ambiente is definitely retro. The American scale seems not to allow recalibration. Once Cuba lodged in the back of the American mind, sometime in the 1920s, its contours were fixed. Whatever has happened later was cut to fit the mold. A Fidel with breast implants is funny, and characters like Tony Montana and Dorita Pérez aren't born every day. But in real life comandantes are not comic and exiles are not exotic.

EIGHT

A Taste of Cuba

The brief British occupation of Cuba in 1762 had one lasting consequence: the introduction of Havanas—and not just Havana—to the British colonies that some years later would become the United States. The man responsible was Israel Putnam ("Old Put" to his friends), a Massachusetts-born officer in the British army, and subsequently an American general in the Revolutionary War, who returned from Cuba with three donkey-loads' worth of cigars and a trunk filled with tobacco seeds. Putnam's booty did not take long to find favor with fellow colonists. Within a few years cigars began to rival pipes as the favored form of tobacco consumption among New England gentry. By the beginning of the nineteenth century, several million "Cuban exiles," as James Russell Lowell called them, were arriving every year.[1] At the same time, factories of homemade cigars began to spring up in Pennsylvania, Connecticut, Rhode Island, and other eastern states. But Havanas were considered far preferable to domestic confections, the so-called stogies, whose name also derived from a toponym, albeit a less exotic one: the Pennsylvania town of Conestoga, site of one of the first American cigar factories. (In Cuba, cigars are called *tabacos; cigarros* are cigarettes.)

Throughout the nineteenth century, the popularity of Cuban cigars, as of cigars generally, continued to surge. The list of cigar aficionados included several presidents and other notables. Like his father, John Quincy Adams, the sixth president, was a connoisseur of fine Havanas, which perhaps explained why he desired Cuba's annexation. His successor, Andrew Jackson, smoked them with his wife. Less fortunate than Jackson, Zachary Taylor, the twelfth president, developed the taste while fighting the Mexican War (as did thousands of other American soldiers), but couldn't light up in the presence of his wife, who was allergic to cigar smoke. Abraham Lincoln is said to have given up his corncob pipe after savoring a Havana. His general in chief, Ulysses S. Grant, smoked two dozen every day. When he ran for president, his campaign song was "A-Smoking His Cigar," which he was probably doing when he died of throat cancer. Unlike Grant, Mark Twain consumed the weed in moderation, "only one cigar at a time."[2] Giving up smoking was so easy, he said, that he did it over and over. Even Uncle Sam was depicted smoking a Havana (fig. 15). In the quintessential "Yankee smoke," Cuba, literally

Fig. 15. "Yankee Smoke." Courtesy Tony Hyman, National Cigar Museum, www.CigarHistory.info.

reduced to atmosphere, forms a smoke wreath around Uncle Sam's head.

The importation of Cuban cigars reached its peak in 1855, as Congress was about to levy a heavy tariff on foreign goods. That year more than three hundred million "Cubans" were shipped to the United States, a figure that has never been equaled. (Fifty years later, Cuban imports were down to fifty-two million; fifty years after that, before Castro's takeover and the subsequent embargo, they had dropped to twenty million.) Aware of who was buying their product, Cuban cigar makers started attaching American names—or what sounded like American names—to their brands: "El Knickerbocker," "La Ladi Franklin," "The Potomag Riber," "Missoury." For their part, American cigar manufacturers bought several million pounds of Cuban leaf every year in an attempt to duplicate the taste of a Havana.

Although the tariff of 1857 led to a drop in legal imports, it made the smuggling of Cubans a thriving business. Just one cigar bust in 1872 netted the authorities a hundred thousand cigars. To outsmart the customs officers, smugglers would hide the contraband in the planks of the ships, behind the mirrors in the staterooms, or under piles of coconuts or sacks of sugar. One enterprising smuggler enclosed the cigars in large rubber bags that he dropped overboard before the ship docked in New York. As the bags were cast adrift, they were picked up by his stateside confederates. The "rubber-bag game," as it was called, went on for years, until the authorities got wise and began inspecting Havana-bound ships *before* they sailed for Cuba—not for cigars but for rubber bags. What happened to the millions of seized cigars is unclear. Like Uncle Sam's Cuba, they probably went up in smoke, one by one.

As domestic cigar production increased, factories opened in such far-flung places as Peru, Indiana (home of the "Havana Rose"); Bethesda, Ohio (cradle of "Spanish Joys"); and Detroit, Michigan (birthplace of the "Velocipede Vuelta Abajo Havanas"). The Ten Years' War in Cuba (1868–1878), which devastated the tobacco crops on the island, caused Cuban imports to plummet, further spurring the growth of the native "seegar." In the 1870s, there were more than three thousand cigar factories in the

United States. Brooklyn alone boasted several hundred, though many of them did not employ more than a few workers and some were no more than *chinchales* (one- or two-man shops). At the Centennial celebration in 1876, dozens of American tobacco companies had exhibitions. Patriotic they may have been, but their outlook was distinctly mañana: "If you think smoking is injurious to your health, stop in the morning" (the slogan of Buffalo-based Henry Breitweiser).

Although condemnation of the weed, "the demoralizing vegetable," was already widespread, promulgated by such groups as the "Clean Living" society, it was not taken all that seriously. In 1866 *Ballou Magazine* publicized the findings of a Dr. Richardson, who concluded that one Havana cigar of good quality contained enough poison to provoke convulsions in a rabbit. A short time later, the *Albion* replied: "The deduction is plain and simple. It is very unhealthy for rabbits to smoke good Havana cigars."[3]

Consumption of cigars and other tobacco products rose steadily throughout the second half of the nineteenth century. In the 1860s annual cigar consumption per person in the United States was twenty-five; twenty years later, that number had doubled. A sign of wealth and status, a fine cigar became a gentleman's accessory, as much a part of his attire as the "smoking jacket" to which it gave rise (in Spanish, tuxedos are still called "smokings"). In a negative twist on the Cuba-as-paradise trope, tobacco-phobes sometimes remarked that the biblical forbidden tree must have been a tobacco plant. What Eve handed to Adam was not a fruit but a Havana.

Nevertheless, Havana sellers and lovers praised their smokes for their therapeutic qualities—a stogie a day keeps the bowels in play—as well as for inducing moods of serene contemplation that smoke out ideas dormant in the brain: "A beacon of thought is the quivering star / That reddens the tip of a fragant cigar."[4] Like the philosophic smoker, the cigar-loving poet also benefited from a Havana:

> Let him who has a mistress to her eyebrow write a sonnet,
> Let the lover of a lily pen a languid ode upon it;
> In such sentimental subject I'm a Philistine and cynic,
> And prefer inspiration drawn from sources nicotinic.[5]

The demand for Cubans produced a lively trade in counterfeits, homegrown cigars impersonating Cuban exiles. The vilest of these, whose manufacture was often attributed to Chinamen, were not made from tobacco but from cabbage leaves and brown wrapping paper dunked in a tobacco-flavored liquid. The plague of phony Havanas—the Jose O'Neills of the cigar industry—led one writer to remark that the genuine article was so rare that it had become "one of the grandest fictions of the day," though few smokers were willing to admit it.[6] But the prevalence of counterfeits only made the real thing even more desirable:

> Real Havana!
> Precious Cigar!

Gentle as manna,
Bright as a star—
Pleasant at fireside,
Cheery on road—
Best of all perfumes
At home or abroad!
Real Havana!
Puff away care—
Blow my misfortunes
Into thin air.[7]

In the first half of the twentieth century, cigar consumption leveled off, and with it the importation of Havanas. Of the 450 million cigars that American men consumed in 1906, less than a tenth came from Cuba, which exported twice as many cigars to England as it did to the States. Since saloons doubled as cigar outlets, Prohibition cut further into cigar sales. By the 1920s, most domestic or imported tobacco was used not for cigars but for cigarettes—the mild, machine-made smoke that replaced cigars for many men and attracted new female smokers. Not only were cigarettes less expensive, but cigar makers, many of them small manufacturers, could not afford the large-scale advertising campaigns of cigarette companies like American Tobacco. During the Great Depression, when real Havanas became unaffordable to most Americans, cigars continued to lose ground to cigarettes.

Yet the mystique of Cuban tobacco remained undiminished. As early as the mid-1800s, U.S. manufacturers began to roll cigars made entirely from Cuban leaf. These American-born Cubans, which came to be called "Clear Havanas," cost less to make and avoided the tariffs on imports. In the 1920s, more Clear Havanas were made in two weeks in Tampa—long a cigar-making center and at this time the "Smoke Capital of the World," home of the Hav-A-Tampa and other popular brands—than were imported in a whole year from Cuba. In 1932, after the Cuban cigar workers' union refused to accept wage cuts, La Corona moved its operations to Trenton, New Jersey, where—the manufacturer claimed—it could make the same cigar for one-third the cost. Cigars made with filler from Cuban leaf and wrapper from elsewhere—Connecticut or Sumatra—were also labeled "Havanas," albeit with less justification. Even those made from Cuban-seed tobacco grown stateside claimed the title of Havanas. The widespread practice of calling anything a "Havana" eventually led to a 1924 court ruling that a cigar could not be so labeled unless it were made entirely—filler, binder, and wrapper—of tobacco grown in Cuba.[8] Nonetheless, most cigars made in the United States continued to be packaged in imitation Havana boxes with imitation Havana labels.

A 1926 ad campaign for Muriels, mild cigars that blended Cuban and domestic tobacco, demonstrates how the "Cuba" brand was adapted to American tastes. Introduced at the beginning of the twentieth century, Muriel cigars became notorious for their sexually suggestive ads, particularly the Mae West–inspired slogan, "Why don't you pick me up and smoke me sometime?" (later toned down to: "Why don't you pick one up and smoke it sometime?"). But decades before sultry Edie Adams purred this question in countless TV commercials throughout the 1950s and 1960s, Muriels had been exploiting the comparison of women to cigars famously articulated by Rudyard Kipling: "A woman is only a woman, but a cigar is a Smoke." With Muriel, however, the smoker could have his woman and smoke her too, since the name referred to both: "Just put a flame to her, and you'll be one of her flames."[9] The ads that explained this caption consisted of "leaves" from Muriel's diary, where she recounted her success in persuading smokers to switch from Cubans to her. One ad showed a well-dressed man sitting on the beach next to a girl in a bathing suit, followed by the entry for "Tuesday":

> It was at Palm Beach that we were first introduced. He was a prominent New York banker, and a friend presented me as we were sunning on the beach.
>
> When he first looked at me, I read a challenge in his eyes. It were as though he had said, "You're too demure for me."
>
> For, in cigars, he had long been partial to rich brunettes from Cuba, and I am somewhat different.
>
> But after he had put a match to me, I had him won! For he found the zest he craved in my choice Havana, and with it an ingratiating and sympathetic mildness that only the finest lighter tobaccos can give.
>
> "This is a wonderful cigar," he told my friend. "I know we'll hit it off famously, for it's just the happy medium smoke I've been looking for.

> So the banker was won . . . on the Florida sands.
> Muriel: The Cigar That's Just Right.[10]

As the racially mixed offspring of dark and light, Cuba and America, Muriel possesses the "zest" of the former without losing the "demure" appearance of the latter. Thus, to get her guy Muriel relies on her difference from both the "rich brunettes" of Cuba and the "lighter" shades of the United States. Like maraca musicals or latunes, she offers adventure without risk, pleasure without consequences (even if, in so doing, she provides an endorsement of miscegenation unusual in a racially segregated society). Enjoying "matchless popularity" with all sorts of men, Muriel elsewhere relates how she conquered a polo player, a famous artist, two seniors at Yale, an automobile man from Detroit, and a fan of the New York Giants. Not even Cleopatra, another ad says, had more admirers than Muriel, who captivates men with her "fragrant presence" and "good taste."[11]

The entries from Muriel's diary were complemented by "the confessions of Muriel's lovers," statements by writers and artists extolling their dusky beloved's paradoxical virtue. Drama critic Alan Dale:

> There's just one thing that bothers me about Muriel. . . . While thousands of men, like myself, love her, she manages to be true to everyone. Still I keep on courting Muriel daily for the very good reason that no other cigar gives me the wholesome and balanced comradeship that I get from Muriel. I have tried those very brunettish and expensive Havanas. They are too rich, too

> heavy. . . . And then I switched to the very blonde domestic brands. Tame as corn-silk without even the thrill of the forbidden "behind-the-barn" smoke. So invariably I come back to Muriel, the Happy Medium, with its ideal medley of characterful Havana and soothing lighter leaf.[12]

Cartoonist Clare Briggs, the creator of the "When a Feller Needs a Friend" comic strip, confessing to his "daily trysts" with Muriel:

> I am perfectly willing to let the world know that I have been keeping company with Muriel for years. For when a feller needs a friend, Muriel never fails him. It's the even temper of Muriel that always appeals to me. Not too mild—for Muriel is never insipid. Not too strong or harsh—for Muriel never gets on the nerves. Indeed, Muriel is the most congenial, just-right, first-rate cigar I know. Its whole-souled Havana is nicely balanced with piquant lighter tobaccos—mated like a feast of reason and a flow of wit. It is some cigar! And what a grand and glorious feeling![13]

Once again, these ads invoke racial and cultural stereotypes: while the American leaf makes Muriel "wholesome and balanced," the Cuban leaf prevents her from being "tame" like the bland domestic brands. She is, as another of her lovers put it, "the most gracious of vamps," where the graciousness speaks to her American side, and the vampishness to her inner Cuban. Dating back to the beginning of the twentieth century, the girl on the cigar labels was actually a heavy-set brunette with large hoop earrings and a mantilla. But the girl in the 1920s ads, dressed fashionably in furs or skimpily in a bathing suit, looked every bit like a flapper—the half-Cuban, all-American honey, spicy yet wholesome: the perfect mate. Ever the lover, never the wife, Muriel is equally suited "for the busy hours of the day, for the tranquil nights of pleasure."[14]

Two hundred years after Cuban cigars were brought to America by Old Put, the embargo on Cuban goods enacted by the Kennedy administration put a stop to their entrance. A lover of the leaf ever since his college days, President Kennedy attempted to have cigars exempted from the prohibition but failed. Unwilling to let foreign policy interfere with his smokes, he commissioned his press secretary, Pierre Salinger, to buy up all the H. Upmann Petit Coronas that he could find. A cigar smoker himself, Salinger tracked down eleven hundred of Kennedy's favorite smoke. With the cigars safely in the White House, President Kennedy signed the executive order establishing the embargo. Some time later, when his supply ran out, he would get his Cubans from the British ambassador, who sneaked them in his diplomatic pouch, thereby avoiding detection.

In the decades since, most cigar smokers in the United States, unlike JFK, have had to make do with cigars grown from Cuban seed in Latin America. Although some of the oldest Cuban brands—Partagás, La Gloria Cubana, H. Upmann, Montecristo—still exist, their cigars—now true exiles—are made outside of Cuba. No matter: "Before there was Castro, there was Partagas"—one of the publicity slogans of the brand that originated in Cuba in 1845, which now makes its cigars in the Dominican Republic. (After Castro there has been Partagás also: some of the pre-Castro brands continue to be produced in Cuba by the state-run cigar industry.) As in the nineteenth century, the scarcity of real Havanas has also fueled a thriving business in counterfeits, particularly of the prestigious Cohibas, Fidel's favorite smoke back in the days when he still had fire in him. John Lantigua's thriller, *Ultimate Havana* (2001), offers an entertaining account of the intrigues surrounding the confection and sale of fake Cubans. Not all of the traffic in fake Cubans is underhanded, however: one Nicaraguan manufacturer unabashedly sells "Genuine Counterfeit Cuban Cigars."

Mostly remembered today as a friend of the Fitzgeralds and Hemingways during their Paris years, Gerald Murphy was also an accomplished painter who, at the height of the Roaring Twenties, painted a canvas in homage to Cuba's contribution to that hedonistic decade. Its title notwithstanding, *Cocktail* (1927) has as its centerpiece a half-empty box of Cuban cigars, the seal vouching for their authenticity (fig. 16). Framing the cigars are the implements used in making a cocktail: a corkscrew, a shaker, long-stemmed glasses. And under the cigar Murphy has placed a lime cut in half. A defining ingredient in rum drinks, from daiquiris to mojitos, the lime suggests that the cocktail about to be made will also have a taste of Cuba. Where there's smoke, there's fiery spirits, for the logical complement to a fine Havana is strong drink. As in *Cocktail*, rum and cigars have always gone

Fig. 16. Gerald Murphy, *Cocktail*, 1927, oil on canvas, 29 1/16 x 29 7/8 in. Whitney Museum of American Art, New York; Purchase, with funds from Evelyn and Leonard A. Lauder, Thomas H. Lee and the Modern Painting and Sculpture Committee 95.188; photography by Sheldan C. Collins; copyright Estate of Honoria Murphy Donnelly/Licensed by VAGA, New York, NY.

hand to mouth together. Listen to the Reverend Orin Fowler, an early prohibitionist, in 1833: "Rum drinking will not cease, till tobacco chewing, and tobacco smoking and snuff-taking shall cease."[15]

The most hallowed rum drink of all, of course, is the Cuba Libre—rum and Coke with a slice of lime—a bibulous memorial to Cuban-American intimacy during and after the Cuban-American war against Spain. Legend has it that the drink originated in a bar in Old Havana, the watering hole for off-duty American officers, when a captain ordered Bacardi and Coca-Cola on ice. The captain drank the concoction with such pleasure that it sparked the interest of those around him. The bartender prepared a round, and the Cuba Libre was born. Other versions of its origins also involve Cuba, the Spanish-American War, and American soldiers celebrating the island's independence with the toast "Cuba Libre!" The problem is that Coca-Cola was not widely available in Cuba in 1898. Thus it is likely that the first Cuba Libre was not consumed during the conflict but may indeed have been invented during the subsequent occupation of the island by U.S. troops. After 1902, when Coca-Cola opened its first bottling plant in Cuba, the drink became a favorite with Cubans, who relished the patriotic name, as well as with American tourists, attracted to the familiar taste of Coke. Years later, the novelist Elinor Rice would say of the Cuba Libre: "Yes, the great symbolic drink of Cuba. Coca-Cola and rum. A small distillate of Cuba drowned in a large dose of synthetic Americana."[16] (In the 1960s, exiled Cubans renamed the drink *mentirita*, little lie, since Cuba was not free).

No less popular than the Cuba Libre was the daiquiri ("dy-kee-reé" in Spanish), devised at about the same time, supposedly by an American engineer named Joseph Cox. Not having gin or whiskey to serve a visitor, Cox mixed lime juice, sugar, and local rum in a shaker, with delicious results. Since the drink had no name, the visitor suggested that it be called daiquiri after the nearby mines, located in Eastern Cuba, near the town of Daiquirí. Another version of the drink's origins has it that General William Shafter, commander of the American expedition to Cuba, whose three-hundred-pound figure did not handle the tropical heat well, added the ice to the mixture of sugar, rum, and lime juice that had been consumed by British sailors since the eighteenth century to combat scurvy (hence the nickname "limey").

Medicinal or not, the daiquiri—word as well as drink—quickly caught on in America. Already in 1910 the D.C. area boasted a bar called the Daiquiri Lounge. Complimentary daiquiris were served to Havana passengers on the Pan Am Clippers. Tourists in Santiago de Cuba were greeted by a representative of the Bacardi rum distillery, sometimes by Facundo Bacardí himself, and served free daiquiris. According to Don Facundo, only one woman ever refused to sample his product, though after he persuaded her to have a "lemonade" (which he spiked with rum, thus producing a de facto daiquiri), the lady in question gladly had several servings. In the 1930s, a new type of rayon fabric was baptized the "daiquiri." A light organdy dress was said to be as "frosty as a Havana daiquiri." Ads for fashionable shoes featured "the Daiquiri, a white suede step-in that meets every requirement of the cocktail hour."[17] When the Waring blender was invented, one of its uses was to make a daiquiri with a sherbet consistency.

Ironically, Prohibition was largely responsible for the popularity of Cuban cocktails in the United States. Removing the American corner saloon with its drunken lower-class patrons from the collective consciousness, Prohibition made drinking glamorous as well as domestic. As consumption of alcohol moved into the home, so did Bacardi. One ad counseled: "Before Prohibition Is Effective Your Home Should Be Supplied with Bacardi." But even afterwards, Bacardi was easy enough to find, thanks to Cuba's proximity and the industriousness of bootleggers. Anything that floated was liable to ferry booze across the Florida Straits: yachts, fishing schooners, power boats, even old submarine chasers from World War I. Though lucrative, rum-running was a risky, violent business, with frequent murders and disappearances. One Cuban official washed up on a beach in Nassau with a note sewn to his lower lip: "This was a cop. We don't want no cops here."[18]

It was during the 1920s and 1930s that cocktail hour became an American institution, and cocktail manuals with titles like *The Merry Mixer* (1933) and *So Red the Nose* (1935) were eagerly consulted. Women who would not think of drinking rye could ask for a cocktail, which provided a disguised and fashionably dressed shot of whiskey, gin, or rum. In Hollywood movies, sleek ladies holding long-stemmed cocktail glasses drank alongside their male friends, and in homes all over America life imitated art.

Rum was so much in demand that Adolph Schmitt, the bartender on a Caribbean cruise ship, complained that passengers no longer ordered scotch or rye, insisting instead on such things as daiquiris and rum swizzles.[19] When sales tripled, the Bacardí family built an attractive Art Deco building in Havana, where smiling bartenders arranged cocktails in a row along a gleaming bar. Although during Prohibition advertisements for alcoholic beverages disappeared from American newspapers, Cuban vacations were often promoted as "wet holidays." Uncle Sam, once pictured smoking a Havana, was now shown "Flying to Heaven," hitching a ride to Cuba on the trademark Bacardi bat—evidently not the proverbial bat out of hell.

Once Prohibition ended in 1933, Bacardi and other manufacturers resumed their advertising campaigns in America. "Viva Cuba!" ran one ad, "She gave us Bacardi!" Longchamps Restaurant in New York City, which bragged that it could "out-Havana Havana," listed its offerings of Bacardi cocktails: the "Cuban Special," "The Presidente," the "Bacardi Highball," and the "Cuba Libre Highball." Cora Vermouth offered a recipe for a cocktail called the "Cubano" (rum, gin, and vermouth). Another New York restaurant, Schrafft's, which catered to a female clientele, reminded its patrons that tea time was also cocktail time, and it could be spent getting "a whiff of the tropics."[20] At the 1939 World's Fair, visitors to the Cuban Pavilion could pick up a complimentary cocktail recipe book in the pavilion's exact replica of Sloppy Joe's.

Before Prohibition, a bottle of rum used to last a whole month at the Mayflower Hotel bar in D.C., but after the Eighteenth Amendment was repealed, the bartenders would go through several in just one day. New cocktails with a Cuban connection proliferated: the "Havana Rainbow" (grenadine, anisette, crème de menthe, yellow curaçao, and rum); the "Havana Beach" (pineapple juice, sugar, and rum); the "Havana Yacht Club" (vermouth, apricot brandy, and rum); the "Hotel Nacional" (lime juice, pineapple juice, apricot brandy, and rum); the "Presidente Menocal" (curaçao, dry vermouth, grenadine, and rum); the "Colonel Batista" (vermouth, lime juice, sugar, and rum); the "Bacardi Blossom" (orange and lime juices, nutmeg, sugar, and rum); the "Cuba Reformé" (lime juice, cola, and gin); the "Santiago Nightcap" (orange curaçao, an egg yolk, and rum); the "Remember the Maine" (vermouth, cherry brandy, rye whiskey, and Pernod). *Boothby's World Drinks* (1934) lists recipes for three "Havana" and five "Cuban" cocktails. According to bartender Johnny Brooks, the definitive rum cocktail was the "Cubanola"—almost a meal in itself: rum, grenadine, orange juice, pineapple juice, lemon juice, and egg whites.[21]

After their heyday in the 1920s and 1930s, Cuban cocktails dropped out of favor for several decades, resurfacing in the 1980s as the latest trend in mixed drinks. Nowadays most popular of all is the mojito, the third member in the Cuban trinity of holy spirits, whose full name is *mojito criollo.* Sometimes described as a Cuban cousin to the mint julep, the mojito is said to have been the brainchild of a shipmate of Sir Francis Drake (hence its old name, *draque*). But long before Drake began cruising the Caribbean in search of Spanish galleons, Cuban cane cutters had been mixing sugar, lime juice, *aguardiente* (a high-octane forerunner of rum), and *yerbabuena* (the abundant local variety of mint). When distillers began refining rum to replace the aguardiente, the mojito moved up to Havana bars and nightclubs, where ice and sparkling water were added. In the 1920s, bartenders at La Bodeguita del Medio, originally a small food store that had metamorphosed into a chic tourist bar, lined up tall glasses, filled them with rum, sugar syrup, mint, and soda water, and used a small wooden mallet or "muddler" to squash the flavors together. The famous framed scrawl over La Bodeguita's long mahogany bar, purported to be in Hemingway's hand, attests to the excellence of the confection: "My mojitos in La Bodeguita, my daiquiris in El Floridita."

Because a good mojito is difficult to make (one man's muddler is another man's mess), today it is easy to find mojito-flavored rums or ready-to-drink mojitos (including a ready-to-drink vodka mojito). Even beer has taken on a Cuban flavor in the "Bacardi Silver Mojito," a cloudy-white beverage with a hint of mint and lime. Less outlandish but not any tastier is the doubly Cuban "Martí Mojito," a flavored rum whose launch was timed to coincide with the new millennium. Described as "the official drink of Ricky Ricardo," the Martí Mojito was promoted with a publicity campaign that was a study in stereotypes. In one ad, arrayed in a semicircle alongside a picture of Martí, same- and opposite-sex couples posed for the camera in various stages of undress—an obvious reference to the *jineterismo* prevalent in Cuba over the last twenty years. Although the drink supposedly captured "the soul of Cuba," the ad showcases instead the bodies of Cubans. Add an old man rolling a cigar and a couple of black musicians, and the portrait of the land of rum, rump, and rumba is complete—and "auténtico," with the accent as the final warrant of authenticity. The images made clear that the slogan—"The revolution will start at happy hour"—referred to sexual rather than political revolutions, a message reiterated in another slogan: "The leaders of this revolution are all behind bars."

With the debut of so-called sensory cocktails, Cuban drinks have entered the cyber age. Enjoy a virtual taste of Cuba: blindfolded, you sip a daiquiri while Cuban sones play on an iPod and a waitress spritzes you with "cigar mist" made from syrup and tobacco simmered in water. The whole thing is a "sensory trick to make you think you're in Havana."[22] This was also the trick turned by Martí Mojito. And this has always been the trick. Now as ever, back-of-the-mind Cuba remains an atmospheric effect, a romantic mist, a trick of the senses: smoke and mirages.

Epilogue

ADAMS'S APPLE

Everything for me always comes back to Cuba.
—Lupe Solano in Carolina García-Aguilera's *Havana Heat* (2000)

On April 28, 1823, John Quincy Adams, the secretary of state in the administration of James Monroe, wrote to the American ambassador in Spain:

> There are laws of political as well as physical gravitation; and if an apple severed by the tempest from its native tree cannot choose but fall to the ground, Cuba, forcibly disjoined from its own unnatural connection with Spain, and incapable of self-support, can gravitate only towards the North American Union, which by the same law of nature cannot cast her off from its bosom.[1]

At the time, Spain was in the midst of a civil war between the supporters of King Ferdinand VII, who had returned to the throne after the Napoleonic invaders were driven out in 1814, and those who wanted Spain to move to a less autocratic monarchy. To ensure the continuance of the Bourbon dynasty, post-Napoleonic France had intervened on the side of Ferdinand VII. Although the United States was neutral, it did have an interest in the war's transatlantic repercussions. Economically Cuba was already linked to the United States, which was rapidly becoming its principal trading partner. Geographically Cuba seemed, as Adams noted in the same letter, a part of North America, its shores separated from recently acquired Florida by a distance of fewer than a hundred miles. Like other American politicians, Adams advocated a policy of watchful waiting. As long as Cuba remained in Spanish hands, nothing would be done, but if another nation threatened to take control of the island, the United States was ready to act. This view, which came to be called the No-Transfer Principle, was codified a few weeks after Adams's letter in the Monroe Doctrine, which held that no European power would be allowed to establish new colonies in the Americas.

One of the most egregious documents in the history of Cuban-American relations, this passage has been quoted numberless times. Even Fidel Castro, in an address to the General Assembly of the United Nations in 1960, cited it as evidence of America's long-standing designs on the island. I prefer to see Adams's apple as an emblem, not of American imperialism, which it certainly is, but of the ways in which American culture has invested Cuba with significance. Comparing Cuba to an apple is a transforming act of imagination; it wraps the island in layers of meaning that say more about the apple-craver than about the object itself. After all, apples don't grow in Cuba. That apple is really "a fig" of the American imagination, as *Bold Venture*'s Inspector LaSalle would have said. A fig, that is, a figment, a figure, an invention of the conscious mind that springs from back-of-the-mind fears and desires.

In Adams's view, Cuba, as a free-falling apple, lacks the capacity to direct its course. Less clear is why he regards Cuba's attachment to Spain, its "native tree," as an "unnatural connection." The native is the natural; the two words descend from the same Latin root, *natus*, to be born. In Spanish, to indicate where someone hails from, his or her native ground, one says "natural de . . . ." What does seem unnatural, or at least anomalous, is Cuba's separation from its native tree: the apple drops not because it is ripe but because of a tempest—Spain's civil unrest. (The Spanish-American War, which finally detached Cuba from Spain almost a century later, would turn out to be a tropical storm rather than a European tempest.) Switching from an organic metaphor to one drawn from physics, Adams then forecasts that Cuba, as it plunges to the ground, will gravitate "up" toward the United States, which will be prevented from casting it off because of the same laws of political gravitation. The island's fall is rather an ascension, with the American Union taking Cuba onto its "bosom" much as a mother would embrace a foundling on her doorstep. According to Adams, while it is unnatural for Cuba to be attached to Spain, it is natural for the island to be accepted into the North American Union, with which it does not share language, heritage, or history.

Adams's metaphor suggests that in the back of *his* mind was the biblical story of the Fall, with Cuba playing the part of the desirable yet forbidden fruit. Forbidden because Adams knew that the annexation of Cuba would face, as he put it, "numerous and formidable objections," not least of which was the likelihood of war with Britain. Yet desirable because he believed that Cuba's annexation, which was "verging into maturity" even as he wrote, was indispensable to the integrity of the Union. Along with the other Caribbean islands, Cuba—as he says elsewhere in the letter, resorting again to a fabricated idea of the natural—is a "natural appendage" of the United States.

This view of Cuba obviously contrasts with the one that Cubans have of their homeland. In the 1950s, Cuban children used to learn about the geography of the island in Leví Marrero's *Geografía de Cuba* (1950), the standard text in the island's schoolrooms throughout the 1950s and into the 1960s. The first illustration in the book, "El mundo alrededor de Cuba" (the world around Cuba), shows a map of the world with Cuba at its center (fig. 17). After explaining the map, the caption concludes: "The hemisphere centered in Cuba includes the Americas, Europe except Moscow, and small parts of Africa and Asia. Cuba is the center of gravity of the Americas."[2]

No less a geographical fiction than Adams's apple-appendage,

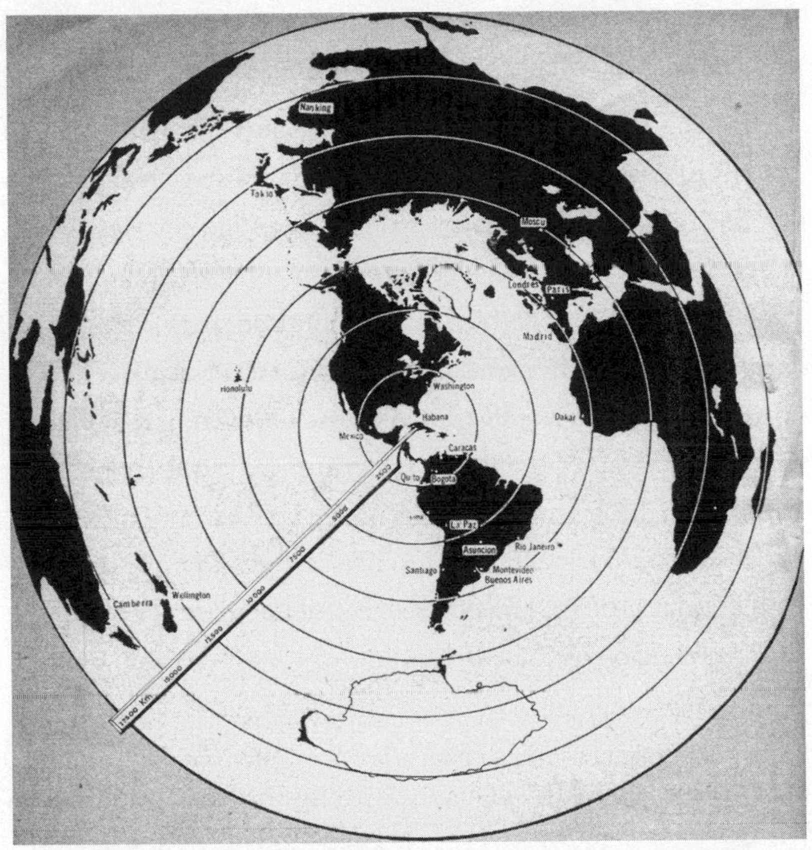

Fig. 17. "El mundo alrededor de Cuba." Leví Marrero, *Geografía de Cuba* (Havana, 1950).

the hemisphere depicted in the map, with Cuba at the center, does convey what Cubans tend to think: that the world revolves around us. Scholars of Cuban culture have called this perspective on Cuba's place in the world *ombliguismo; ombligo* is navel—hence, Cuba is the navel of the planet, and its natives are given to navel-gazing. For a different manifestation of the same idea, think back to the mural that Conrado Massaguer painted for the Cuban Pavilion at the World's Fair: a rumbera surrounded by the leaders of East and West—Cuba on the world stage—all of them hypnotized by the gyrations of her hips (fig. 9). Massaguer's mural could also have been called "The World around Cuba." A line from a song by the Cuban-American performer Willy Chirino sums up ombliguismo or Cuban exceptionalism in four words: *Como Cuba, ni Cuba.* Like Cuba, not even Cuba. That is, Cuba is exceptional even with regard to itself. If islands are exceptions to the rule of continents, Cuba is an exception to an exception, an incontinent rule unto itself.

Back in the 1880s, James Steele had already formed much the same impression of Cubans:

> The island idea is that Cuba is a continent, perhaps not literally, but in effect. Havana *and* New York are capitals of the world. They are reluctantly willing to divide the honors. A certain inner consciousness of the Cuban islander makes him believe that only adverse circumstances, such as want of money or want of knowledge, prevents every man from emigrating to Cuba. The idea of cold is terrible to him, and he fancies it must be so to every human. It is a climactic egotism especially islandic in form. He does not say so, but nevertheless believes, that in climate, soil, intelligence, wealth, and *size* his country leads the world.[3]

Contemporary corroboration of Steele: before the collapse of the Soviet Union, Cuban exiles liked to say that their homeland was the largest country in the world: it had its territory in the

Caribbean, its government in Moscow, and its population in Miami. The mediocre joke was popular because, at some level, it ratified our sense of Cuba's importance.

A corollary of ombliguismo is the belief that Cuba is everywhere—not only the center but the circumference of the universe, somewhat like the god of medieval philosophers. For Cubans, it's all, and always, about us. This book, which has detected Cuban magic dust—bilongo—in the nooks and crannies of American culture, may well be another example of the Cuban inclination to find Cuba in the most unlikely places. Take the movie *The Blob*, mentioned in an earlier chapter. It is widely thought that the fad of science-fiction films in the 1950s reflected Americans' fear of communism, the Red Scare. But what if the movie were a reaction not to communism but to Cubanism? When *The Blob* was released in October 1958, the success of the Castro-led revolt was very much in doubt, but things Cuban, as we have seen, had been items of Americana for many years, and never as visibly or audibly as in the 1950s. Thus, it may not be trivial that the movie's theme song, composed by Burt Bacharach and Mack David, is a mambo—one of those Cuban imports that had invaded the nation just a few years earlier. In the lyric, the Blob is described as "creeping and leaping" and "gliding and sliding" across the floor. What is this if not a description of someone doing the mambo? A gelatinous sibling of Cuban Pete, the Blob mamboes across Pennsylvania, engulfing anyone in its path.

Notice, also, that the Blob's Achilles heel is its intolerance to cold. If the Blob came from outer space, and particularly if it's a symbol of Soviet expansionism, the logical vulnerability would be to heat, not to cold. It is Cubans, as Steele points out, that find cold intolerable. When the Blob is finally disposed of by being dropped in the Arctic, this fate evokes every Cuban's worst nightmare: freezing to death. No, the Blob did not fall from another planet; it gravitated up from the south, as Adams would have had it. From the ombligo perspective, the Blob is Cuban—a Cublob—which is why it looks exactly like guava jelly. And so the subject is not the Red Scare but the Guava Panic. A supplement to Adams's famous letter, *The Blob* offers an alternative metaphor for Cuba: deadly guava rather than forbidden apple.

Is this understanding of *The Blob* divination or hallucination?

The second illustration in my old geography textbook also shows Cuba, but now "seen from the North": "Cuba vista desde el norte" (fig. 18). Since in Cuban slang "el norte" is the United States, the caption could also be translated: "Cuba seen from the United States." Although the map purports to illustrate the island's strategic position as the gateway to the Americas, there is something a little ominous in the projection, which views Cuba from an elevated point somewhere in the middle of the United States, suggesting that the island is not only being looked at but watched over. Uncannily, the map includes the southern tip of Florida, as if that part of the United States did not belong to "the North"—a harbinger of things and people to come. (By the same

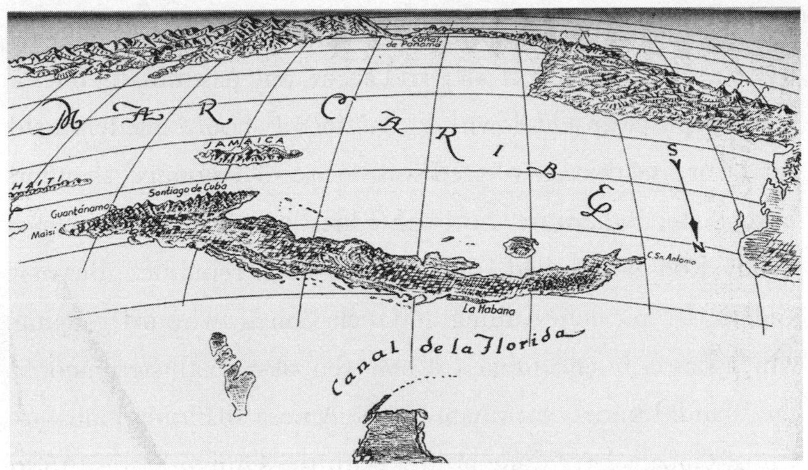

Fig. 18. "Cuba vista desde el norte." Leví Marrero, *Geografía de Cuba* (Havana, 1950).

token, the exclusion of Moscow from the Cuban hemisphere in the first map seems, in retrospect, tragically wrong.)

Put the two maps together and what you have is self-consciousness in two senses: consciousness of how you see yourself and of how others see you. In Cuba's case, the two go together, for an abiding anxious awareness of the Colossus to the north has shaped Cuban self-consciousness ever since the first stirrings of national feeling two centuries ago. In the course of this book I have surveyed, as a map surveys, what "el norte" sees when it looks at Cuba. At the same time, I have discussed the often eager participation of Cubans in American projections. Americans think that Cuba is special, and Cubans agree: the island is the apple of all our eyes.

As a Cuban, maybe I should be distressed by America's inability to see my country clearly and accurately (seen from *el norte*, Cuba appears upside down, doesn't it?). I should condemn the caricatures of the city where I was born and denounce, as others have done, American shortsightedness in dealing with what Teddy Roosevelt called "that infernal little republic." But as a Cuban, I can't help smiling at Uncle Sam's awkward groping, which has only encouraged *cubano*-centrism, both here and on the island. I know that whatever the Americans have done with Cuba, Cubans have done no less with the United States. And I know too that Cuba's troubles, which are many and continuing, have far more to do with how Cubans have treated one another than with how Americans have treated us.

In the third of the Thin Man movies, *Another Thin Man* (1939), Nick and Nora find themselves at the West Indies Club, a Latin-themed nightspot whose décor runs to palm-thatched huts and sultry señoritas. The featured act is the dancing team of René and Estela, who specialize in an elaborate rumba routine called "el tornillo," the screw, so labeled because the male dancer gyrates slowly on one leg, as if screwing himself into the floor. After René has finished swiveling to the strains of "Siboney," Nick strikes up a conversation with a couple of the regulars about a thug named Church who has just returned from Cuba, or so Nick thinks. One of the regulars happens to know Church well. Church has been to Cuba, he counters, pointing around, but "only if you call this Cuba."

For two hundred years, you—we—have indeed called this type of place, this magical locale, Cuba. Based in fact and built on fiction, a compact of truth and imagination, Cuba has intrigued, enamored, fascinated, and frustrated Americans no less than it has Cubans themselves. Through it all, the Havana Habit has endured. It is surely the case that the story told in these pages is not yet over.

Notes

INTRODUCTION

1. Peter Watrous, "A Song Sails Forth from Cuba," *New York Times*, Aug. 21, 1997, C11–C16.
2. Michael Wood, *America in the Movies* (1975; New York: Columbia University Press, 1989), xiii.
3. Victor Segalen, *Essay on Exoticism: An Aesthetics of Diversity*, trans. Yaël Rachel Schlick (1955; Durham, NC: Duke University Press, 2002).
4. William Henry Hurlbert, *Gan-Eden; or, Pictures of Cuba* (Boston: John P. Jewett, 1854), 9; James W. Steele, *Cuban Sketches* (New York: G. P. Putnam's Sons, 1881), 15.
5. Consuelo Hermer and Marjorie May, *Havana Mañana: A Guide to Cuba and the Cubans* (New York: Random House, 1941), 47.
6. Dorothy M. Figueira, *The Exotic: A Decadent Quest* (Albany: State University of New York, 1994), 2–3; Joseph Hergesheimer, *San Cristóbal de La Habana* (1920; New York: Alfred A. Knopf, 1927), 252.
7. "For Gourmets: Havana's Fare," *New York Times*, Sept. 3, 1939, D9.
8. Robert D. Heinl, "Dial Flashes," *Washington Post*, Nov. 22, 1930, 10; Kay Ware, "Way Proposed to Banish Lone Turkey Eater," *Washington Post*, Nov. 14, 1934, 10; Mary Harris, "Ringside Table," *Washington Post*, May

10, 1940, 10; "Plans Advance for Debutante Spanish Ball," *Washington Post*, Mar. 13, 1932, S2.

9. "Bolero Ball Opens Romany Club Season," *New York Times*, Oct. 30, 1932, 34; "Rhumba Dominates in Roosevelt Grill," *New York Times*, Sept. 29, 1934, 12.
10. Erna Fergusson, *Cuba* (New York: Alfred A. Knopf, 1946), 10.
11. "Cuba Rejoices in a Good Supply of 'Bilongo,'" *Washington Post*, Apr. 15, 1951, F7.
12. René Wellek, *Concepts of Criticism* (New Haven: Yale University Press, 1963), 284.

ONE
America's Smartest City

Epigraph: Audax Minor, "The Race Track," *New Yorker*, Jan. 27, 1940, 44.

1. Advertisement for Ward Line Cruises to Havana, *New York Times*, July 24, 1932, xxii; advertisement by Cuban Tourist Commission, *New Yorker*, Dec. 1, 1928, 91.
2. Frederic Remington, "Havana, 1899," in *The Reader's Companion to Cuba*, ed. Alan Ryan (New York: Harcourt Brace, 1997), 66; Karl K. Kitchen, "Wet Message from Garcia," *Boston Daily Globe*, Mar. 7, 1920, E2.
3. William Cullen Bryant, *Letters of a Traveller; or, Notes of Things Seen in Europe and America* (New York: G. P. Putnam, 1850), 373.
4. Bob Racket, "A New-Yorker in Havana," *Spirit of the Times: A Chronicle of the Turf, Agriculture, Field Sports, Literature and the Stage*, Feb. 26, 1848, 6; Alexander Gilmore Caltell, *To Cuba and Back in Twenty-Two Days* (Philadelphia: Times Printing House, 1874), 13.
5. "A Glance at Havana," *Putnam's Monthly Magazine of American Literature, Science, and Art* 1, no. 2 (1853), 188, 190; "Description of the Island of Cuba," *Christian Watchman*, May 27, 1820, 1C; "How They Live in Havana," *Putnam's Monthly Magazine of American Literature, Science, and Art* 1, no. 3 (1853), 290.
6. James Steele, *Cuban Sketches* (New York: G. P. Putnam's Sons, 1881), 219, 16; "How They Live in Havana," 291; Racket, "New-Yorker in Havana," 27; F.C.N., "A Letter from Havana," *Lippincott's Magazine of Popular Literature and Science* (April 1875), 511; Richard Henry Dana, Jr., *To Cuba and Back: A Vacation Voyage* (Boston: Ticknor and Fields, 1859), 71.
7. James W. Steele, *Cuban Sketches* (New York: G. P. Putnam's Sons, 1881), 40.

8. "Cuba under the Flag of the United States," *New York Sun*, July 23, 1847; Walt Whitman, *I Sit and Look Out: Editorials from the Brooklyn Daily Times*, ed. Emory Holloway and Vernolian Schwarz (New York: Columbia University Press, 1932), 157.
9. Maturin M. Ballou, *Due South; or, Cuba Past and Present* (New York: Houghton, Mifflin, 1897), 218; William Henry Hurlbert, *Gan-Eden; or, Pictures of Cuba* (Boston: John P. Jewett, 1854), 180.
10. "An Ocean Picnic," *Harper's Bazaar*, Mar. 9, 1872, 178; Alfred Ashton, "A Peep at Havana," *Manhattan* 1, no. 2 (1883), 126.
11. Edmund Wilson, *The Shores of Light: A Literary Chronicle of the Twenties and Thirties* (New York: Farrar, Straus and Young, 1952), ix; James Gould Cozzens, *The Son of Perdition* (1929; Cleveland: Tower Books, 1942), 225.
12. Karl K. Kitchen, "Wet Message from Garcia," *Boston Daily Globe*, Mar. 7, 1920, E2; Bruce Bliven, "And Cuba for the Winter," *New Republic*, Feb. 29, 1928, 64.
13. Advertisement for the Sevilla Biltmore Hotel, *Life*, Jan. 13, 1927, 34.
14. Beverly Smith, Jr., "To Cuba with Cal," *Saturday Evening Post*, Feb. 1, 1958, 78; "to the Cuban Spirit of Liberty": *Life*, Jan. 19, 1928, 6; Newman Levy, "Ode to Havana," *Life*, Jan. 19, 1928, 7.
15. Charles G. Booth, *Mr. Angel Comes Aboard* (Harrisburg, PA: Military Service, 1944), 30.
16. Hoagy Carmichael, *The Stardust Road and Sometimes I Wonder: The Autobiographies of Hoagy Carmichael* (New York: Da Capo, 1999), 113–114.
17. Sydney A. Clark, *Cuban Tapestry* (New York: National Travel Club, 1936), 98; "national cocktail route" quoted in "Says Monte Carlo Is Rising in Havana," *New York Times*, Dec. 11, 1919, 9.
18. G. L. Morrill, *Sea Sodoms: A Sinical Survey of Haiti, Santo Domingo, Porto Rico, Curacao, Venezuela, Guadeloupe, Martinique, Cuba* (Minneapolis, MN: Pioneer, 1921), 177.
19. William Henry Hurlbert, *Gan-Eden, or Pictures of Cuba* (Boston: John P. Jewett, 1854), 236; Joseph Hergesheimer, *San Cristóbal de Habana* (1920; New York: Alfred A. Knopf, 1927), 43; Sir Basil Thompson, "The Paris of the Caribbean," *Travel* 42, no. 2 (1923), 4; Sydney Clark, *All the Best in Cuba* (New York: Dodd, Mead, 1946), 65; Consuelo Hermer and Marjorie May, *Havana Mañana: A Guide to Cuba and the Cubans* (New York: Random House, 1941), 3–4; Sydney A. Clark, *Cuban Tapestry* (New York: National Travel Club, 1936), 23–39; "nothing will be done" quoted in "Havana's Mayor Voices Welcome," *Wall Street Journal*, Dec. 14, 1931, 18.

20. Leigh White, "Havana," *Saturday Evening Post*, Mar. 31, 1951, 24; James W. Steele, *Cuban Sketches* (New York: G.P. Putnam's Sons, 1881), 22; Robert Fortune, "Sin—with a Rhumba Beat!" *Stag* 1, no. 5 (1950), 22.

TWO
A Little Rumba Numba

Epigraph: *Life*, November 1933, 20.

1. "Cuban Fireball (Songs)," *Variety*, Mar. 14, 1951, 7; "Havana Rose (Songs)," *Variety*, Sept. 9, 1951, 6; Cole Porter quoted in Richard G. Hubler, *The Cole Porter Story* (Cleveland, OH: World, 1965), 52; John Storm Roberts, *The Latin Tinge: The Impact of Latin American Music on the United States*, 2nd ed. (New York: Oxford University Press, 1999), 83.
2. "Cuban Invasion," *Time*, Feb. 23, 1931; "Fritzi Scheff Sings to Palace Plaudits," *New York Times*, Apr. 28, 1930, 27.
3. *Will Rogers' Daily Telegrams*, Vol. 2: *The Hoover Years, 1929–1931*, ed. James M. Smallwood and Steven K. Gragert (Stillwater: Oklahoma State University Press, 1978), 232.
4. L. Wolfe Gilbert, *Without Rhyme or Reason* (New York: Vantage, 1956), 166; Hoagy Carmichael, *The Stardust Road and Sometimes I Wonder: The Autobiographies of Hoagy Carmichael* (New York: Da Capo, 1999), 140; Burton Lane quoted in Arnold Shaw, *Let's Dance: Popular Music in the 1930s*, ed. Bill Willard (New York: Oxford University Press, 1998), 33.
5. Quoted in Theodore S. Beardsley, "Enric Madriguera: Caribbean Music (1920–1941)," liner notes, *Enric Madriguera, 1920–1941* CD (Harlequin, 1994); *Life*, August 1934, 17; Arthur Murray, *How to Become a Good Dancer* (New York: Simon and Schuster, 1954), 111; "Aim to Standardize Ballroom Dancing," *New York Times*, Nov. 10, 1935, 38; "Dance Instructors See Doom of 'Swing,'" *New York Times*, Aug. 27, 1936, 16.
6. "R. P. Shuler Takes Rap at Rhumba," *Los Angeles Times*, July 23, 1931, 3; advertisement for Saks Fifth Avenue, *New York Times*, Oct. 2, 1941, 8; "Rhumba Gives New Silhouette to Style Mart," *Washington Post*, Jan. 22, 1934, 11.
7. Helen Lawrenson, "Latins Are Lousy Lovers," *Esquire*, October 1936, 36–37, 198. A snippet: "God knows the Cuban man spends enough time on the subject of sex. He devotes his life to it. He talks it, dreams it, reads, it, sings it, dances it, eats it, sleeps it—does everything but do it. The last is not literally true, but it is a fact that they spend far more time in words than in action. Sitting in their offices, rocking on the sidewalk

in front of their clubs, drinking at cafés, they talk hour after hour about sex. . . . They telephone each other at their offices during business hours to describe in minute detail a new conquest. According to them, they always had their first affair at the age of two. This may account for their being worn out at twenty-three." One can understand why the Cuban government confiscated from Havana newsstands the copies of the *Esquire* issue in which the article appeared. Twenty years after the Latin Lover piece, Lawrenson returned to Havana to report on Cuban women, for whom (according to Lawrenson) "the simplest acts of taking a shower or doing their nails assume the erotic aura of a rite performed by apprentice courtesans in some ancient temple of Venus. They live for love, and sometimes by it, and the result is a city whose mood of sensuous hedonism is irresistibly contagious to the stranger within its gates." Lawrenson, "The Sexiest City in the World," *Esquire*, February 1956, 31. It seems that Lawrenson was something of an expert on sexposés; she also published another notorious piece, "Why Nice Girls Abandon Underwear," in *Swank* in 1956.

8. John Martin, "We Trade Fox Trot for Rumba," *New York Times*, Feb. 6, 1944, 23.
9. Quoted in Arnold Shaw, *Let's Dance: Popular Music in the 1930s*, ed. Bill Willard (New York: Oxford University Press, 1998), 188.

THREE
Music for the Eyes

1. "Films' Latin-American Cycle Find Congarumba Displacing Swing Music," *Variety*, Nov. 6, 1940, 1, 22; "Argentina Bans U.S. Film for False View of the Nation," *New York Times*, May 5, 1941, 8; Brian O'Neil, "The Demands of Authenticity: Addison Durland and Hollywood's Latin Image," in *Classic Hollywood, Classic Whiteness*, ed. Daniel Bernardi (Minneapolis: University of Minnesota Press, 2001).
2. Bosley Crowther, "The Screen in Review," *New York Times*, Mar. 29, 1947, 21, review of *Carnival in Costa Rica*.
3. Bosley Crowther, "The Screen," *New York Times*, Nov. 8, 1941, 11, review of *Week-End in Havana*.
4. Although Romero often played native-born Latin Americans or Spaniards—including a different kind of conquistador, Hernán Cortés, in *Captain from Castille*—he was born in New York City of Cuban parents, the grandson of no less a personage than José Martí. It was an open

secret in Hollywood that, in spite of his Latin Lover image, Romero was gay.

5. Michael Wood, *America in the Movies* (1975; New York: Columbia University Press, 1989), 33.
6. John Martin, "We Trade Fox Trot for Rumba," *New York Times*, Feb. 6, 1944, 23.
7. Consuelo Hermer and Marjorie May, *Havana Mañana: A Guide to Cuba and the Cubans* (New York: Random House, 1941), 224.

FOUR
Mad for Mambo

1. Jack Kerouac, *On the Road* (1957; New York: Viking, 1997), 293.
2. Marshall Stearns, *The Story of Jazz* (New York: Oxford University Press, 1956), 182; Bill Smith, "Perez Prado Ork," *Billboard*, Aug. 7, 1954, 46–47.
3. "The Mambo," *Time*, Apr. 9, 1951, 38; Kap., "Band Review, Perez Prado," *Variety*, Aug. 29, 1951; Ralph J. Gleason, "Swinging the Golden Gate: Prado's West Coast Tour Proving a Huge Success," *Downbeat*, Oct. 5, 1941, 15.
4. Barbara Squier Adler, "The Mambo and the Mood," *New York Times Magazine*, Sept. 11, 1951, 20; Nat Hentoff, "Prado Tells How Mambo Made It but Not How He Makes It Tick," *Downbeat*, Dec. 1, 1954, 3; Lydia Hinde, "Mambo King Explains New Craze," *Dancing Star* 5, no. 1 (1955), 8–9.
5. Barbara Squier Adler, "The Mambo and the Mood," *New York Times Magazine*, Sept. 11, 1951, 20, 22; "Mambo King," *Ebony*, September 1951, 45–58, 46; "Pérez Prado Shines on Coast," *Downbeat*, Jan. 13, 1954, 28.
6. Albert Butler and Josephine Butler, "Mambo Today," *Dance* 27 (December 1953), 52; Mrs. Arthur Murray, "What the Heck Is the Mambo," *Down Beat*, Dec. 1, 1954, 2; Robert Fontaine, "Ole!" *Saturday Evening Post*, Aug. 13, 1955, 38.
7. Walter Waltham, "Mambo: The Afro-Cuban Dance Craze," *American Mercury* 74 (January 1952), 14–20; "Uncle Sambo, Mad for Mambo," *Life*, Dec. 20, 1954, 15.
8. Ernest Borneman, "Mambo '54," *Melody Maker*, Jan. 1, 1955, 5; "Mambo Fever Hits Peak in Music Biz, with More to Come," *Variety*, Oct. 20, 1954, 121.

9. Smith, "Perez Prado Ork," 46–47; "Night Club Reviews," *Variety*, Aug. 4, 1954, 52; Ernest Borneman, "Big Mambo Business," *Melody Maker*, Sept. 11, 1934.
10. "Darwin and the Mambo," *Time*, Sept. 6, 1954, 34.
11. Quoted in "New Terps Bet Hot-Cha Cha, *Variety*, Mar. 9, 1954; "Cha-Cha-Cha Old Hat Says Pérez Prado," *Billboard*, Sept. 10, 1955.
12. Quoted in Ken Emerson, *Always Music in the Air* (New York: Viking, 2005), 125–126.

FIVE
Cuba in Apt. 3-B

1. Jack Gould, "Why Millions Love Lucy," *New York Times Magazine*, Mar. 1, 1953, 16. The titles of the episodes and the dates when they were first shown are taken from Bart Andrews, *The "I Love Lucy" Book* (New York: Doubleday, 1976).
2. Cecilia Ager, "Desilu, or from Gags to Riches," *New York Times Magazine*, Apr. 30, 1958, 40; http://www.museum.tv/archives/etv/I/htmlI/ilovelucy/ilovelucy.htm.
3. *I Love Lucy* was the first American TV program to show a pregnant woman. When the representatives of Philip Morris, the show's sponsor, objected to Lucy's pregnancy, Arnaz sent off an angry letter to Alfred E. Lyons, the head of the cigarette company. In reply, Lyons sent a one-sentence memo to the executives in charge of the program: "Don't fuck around with the Cuban." The word "pregnant" was never used, however; instead, Lucy was "expectant."
4. Walter Ames, "Arnaz Bringing New Words to Hollywood," *Los Angeles Times*, Dec. 16, 1951, E8.
5. Desi Arnaz, *A Book* (New York: William Morrow, 1976), 270.

SIX
Dirges in Bolero Time

1. Wallace Stevens, "A Word with José Rodríguez-Feo," in *The Collected Poems of Wallace Stevens* (New York: Knopf, 1954), 333; Elinor Rice, *Action in Havana* (New York: Duel, Sloan and Pearce, 1940), 33.
2. Cornell Woolrich, *The Black Path of Fear* (1944; New York: Ballantine Books, 1982), 5; Dashiell Hammett, *Selected Letters, 1921–1960*, ed. Richard Layman and Julie M. Rivett (Washington, DC: Counterpoint,

2001), 476; Francis and Richard Lockridge, *Voyage into Violence* (Philadelphia: J. B. Lippincott, 1956), 154.

3. H. I. Phillips, "Dumm and Dummer," *Washington Post*, Nov. 2, 1930, 16; Consuelo Hermer and Marjorie May, *Havana Mañana: A Guide to Cuba and the Cubans* (New York: Random House, 1941), xii.
4. *Hollywood Reporter*, Apr. 22, 1949, 3–4.
5. George Harmon Coxe, *Murder in Havana* (New York: Dell, 1943), 49, 20.
6. Like Sylvester's novel, *We Were Strangers* was based on incidents surrounding the assassination of Clemente Vázquez Bello, the president of the Cuban senate, who was killed in September 1932 as he was leaving the Havana Yacht Club. Hatched by an anti-Machado terrorist group, the plan was to explode a bomb during Vázquez Bello's funeral, which would be attended by Machado and other top government officials. When a gardener discovered three hundred pounds of explosives buried among the tombs in the Colón cemetery, the funeral was moved to the Vázquez Bello family plot in the Santa Clara province, and the plan was foiled. Machado's overthrow did not occur until a year later.

SEVEN
Comic Comandantes, Exotic Exiles

1. John Leonard, "Che!—The Making of a Movie Revolutionary," *New York Times*, Dec. 8, 1968, 62.
2. Anne Richardson Roiphe, *Up the Sandbox* (Greenwich, CT: Fawcett Crest Books, 1972), 73.
3. Mel Arrighi, *The Castro Complex: A Comedy in Two Acts* (New York: Dramatists Play Service, 1971); Herbert L. Matthews, "Cuban Rebel Is Visited in Hideout," *New York Times*, Feb. 24, 1957, 34; Matthews, "Cuba Seen on Eve of Grave Events," *New York Times*, Mar. 23, 1958, E10.
4. "Powell Defends Acts of Castro in Cuba," *Atlanta Daily World*, Jan. 29, 1959, 1; Norman Mailer, "An Open Letter to Fidel Castro," *Village Voice*, Apr. 27, 1961, 14; "Humanist Abroad," *Time*, May 4, 1959, 27–28; Abbie Hoffman, *Revolution for the Hell of It* (New York: Dial, 1968), 13.
5. Andrew Tully, *A Race of Rebels* (New York: Simon and Schuster, 1960), 157; Mary Morris, *House Arrest* (New York: Doubleday, 1996), 36; Stephen Hunter, *Havana* (New York: Simon and Schuster, 2003), 185.
6. Marc Morano, "Critics Assail Fidel Castro's 'Sickening' Grip on Hollywood Celebs," CNSnews.com, Dec. 17, 2002, http://www.globalexchange

.org/countries/americas/cuba/uscuba/529html; Richard R. Lingeman, "The Greeks Had a Word for It—But What Does It Mean?" *New York Times Magazine*, Aug. 4, 1968, 28.

7. Edna Buchanan, *Act of Betrayal* (New York: Hyperion, 1996), 13.
8. The disclaimer: "*Scarface* is a fictional account of the activities of a small group of ruthless criminals. The characters do not represent the Cuban American community and it be would erroneous and unfair to suggest that they do. The vast majority of Cuban / Americans have demonstrated a dedication, vitality and enterprise that has [sic] enriched the American scene."
9. Christine Bell, *The Perez Family* (New York: Harper Perennial, 1991), 24.
10. Gail Godwin, *Queen of the Underworld* (New York: Ballantine Books, 2007), 46; Joan Didion, *Miami* (New York: Simon and Schuster, 1987), 33.
11. Didion, *Miami*, 23, 139; Jan Morris, "Miami Libre," *Vanity Fair*, June 1983, 71, 76.
12. Carolina García-Aguilera, *A Miracle in Paradise* (New York: Avon, 1999), 93.
13. Bob Herbert, "Lost in the Shouting," *New York Times*, Apr. 3, 2000, 21;Judy Mann, "Cuban Exiles' Obsession Is Catching," *Washington Post*, Jan. 26, 2000, C14; Nancy Gibbs, "I Love My Child," *Time*, Apr. 17, 2000, 25; David Rieff, "The Exiles' Last Hurrah," *New York Times*, Apr. 2, 2000, WK15.
14. Advertisement for San Cristobal Travel, *Hispania* 85, no. 2 (2002), xxii; advertisement for Uniropa S.E.H. Inc., *Hispania* 84, no. 4 (2001), xx; advertisement for Spanish Travel Study Programs of California State University, *Hispania* 84, no. 3 (2001), xxii.
15. "Cuban Girls, Sex in Cuba and Jineteras," http://sexincuba.com.
16. Francine Prose, "Splashy, Flashy Miami," *New York Times*, Mar. 1, 1992, 59.

EIGHT
A Taste of Cuba

1. Thanking Charles Eliot Norton for a box of Havanas, Lowell wrote: "But imp, O Muse, a stronger wing / Mount, leaving self below, and sing / What thoughts these Cuban exiles bring!" *Letters of James Russell Lowell*, ed. Charles Eliot Norton (New York: Harper and Brothers, 1894), 207.
2. Mark Twain, "Advice to Girls," *Mark Twain's Speeches* (New York: Harper and Brothers, 1910), 107.
3. "Smoking: A Few Words between the Whiffs," *Round Table*, June 11,

1864, 402; "To Smokers," *Ballou's Monthly Magazine* 23, no. 1 (1866), 75; "Advice to Rabbits," *Albion*, Feb. 10, 1866, 70.

4. "Smoking: A Few Words between the Whiffs," 402.
5. Arthur W. Gundry, "My Cigar," in *Pipe and Pouch: The Smoker's Book of Poetry*, comp. Joseph Knight (Boston: H. M. Caldwell, 1894), 3.
6. "Random Notes," *Every Saturday: A Journal of Choice Reading*, Feb. 18, 1871, 158.
7. *Everybody's Album: A Humorous Collection of Tales, Quips, Quirks, Anecdotes and Facetiae*, Aug. 1, 1836, 100.
8. "Bars Havana Label on Other Tobaccos," *New York Times*, Feb. 16, 1924, 22.
9. Advertisement for Muriel Cigars, "Muriel Has More Admirers Than Cleopatra Ever Had!" *New York Times*, Mar. 2, 1926, 16.
10. Advertisement for Muriel Cigars, "Leaves from Muriel's Diary," *New York Times*, Mar. 9, 1926, 17.
11. Advertisement for Muriel Cigars, *New York Times*, Mar. 2, 1926, 16.
12. Advertisement for Muriel Cigars, "The Confessions of Muriel's Lovers," *New York Times*, Mar. 28, 1925, 11.
13. Advertisement for Muriel Cigars, *New York Times*, Apr. 9, 1925, 26.
14. Advertisement for Muriel Cigars, *New York Times*, June 4, 1925, 16; advertisement for Muriel Cigars, "There's a Lover of Muriel for Every Light on Broadway," *New York Times*, Sept. 15, 1925, 18.
15. Quoted in Roberts, *The Story of Tobacco in America* (New York: Alfred A. Knopf, 1949), 107.
16. Elinor Rice, *Action in Havana* (New York: Duell, Sloan and Pearce, 1940), 281.
17. "Mr. Bacardi," *New Yorker*, Feb. 9, 1929, 14–15; advertisement for Woodward and Lothrop, "Gay Pretender," *Washington Post*, Apr. 5, 1937, 4; advertisement for Bonwit Teller, "White Embroidered Organdy," *New York Times*, May 30, 1937, 5; advertisement for I. Miller Shoes, "Cruise Indispensables," *New York Times*, Jan. 14, 1934, 6.
18. Advertisement for Bacardi Rum, *New York Times*, Jan. 22, 1919, 4; "Gun Cay Is Nassau's Rival as Port for Rum Runners," *Washington Post*, Aug. 23, 1921, 5.
19. "Americans Demand Variety in Drinks, Liner's Mixer Says," *New York Times*, Feb. 23, 1927, 3.
20. Advertisement for Bacardi Rum, *Life*, June 1934, 39; advertisement for

Longchamps Restaurant, *New York Times*, May 12, 1936, 2; advertisement for Schrafft's, *New York Times*, Oct. 2, 1936, 7.

21. Dudley Harmon, "Fashions in Drinks Change as Frequently as Style," *Washington Post*, July 18, 1937, B4;Johnny Brooks, *My Thirty-Five Years behind Bars* (New York: Exposition, 1954), 87.
22. Jonathan Miles, "You Can't See It to Believe It," *New York Times*, Aug. 17, 2008, 13.

EPILOGUE

Epigraph: Carolina García-Aguilera, *Havana Heat* (New York, William Morrow, 2000), 24.

1. John Quincy Adams, *The Writings of John Quincy Adams*, ed. Worthington Chauncey Ford, vol. 7 (New York: Macmillan, 1917), 373.
2. "El hemisferio centrado en Cuba incluye las Américas, Europa, excepto Moscú, y pequeñas partes de Africa y Asia. En Cuba está el centro de gravedad de las Américas." Leví Marrero, *Geografía de Cuba* (Havana: Talleres Tipográficos Alfa, 1950), 2.
3. James Steele, *Cuban Sketches* (New York: G.P. Putnam's, 1881), 198.

Index

Page numbers in italics refer to illustrations.